Elegant Hotels

of *Europe*

Elegant Hotels
of Europe

Wendy Black and **HOTELS**

ARCHITECTURE & INTERIOR DESIGN LIBRARY

An Imprint of
PBC International, Inc.

Distributor to the book trade in the United States and Canada
Rizzoli International Publications Inc.
300 Park Avenue South
New York, NY 10010

Distributor to the art trade in the United States and Canada
PBC International, Inc.
One School Street
Glen Cove, NY 11542

Distributor throughout the rest of the world
Hearst Books International
1350 Avenue of the Americas
New York, NY 10019

Library Of Congress Cataloging–in–Publication Data

Black, Wendy.
  Elegant hotels of Europe / by Wendy Black and Hotels magazine.
      p.   cm.
  Includes indexes.
  ISBN 0–86636–227–4
  1. Hotels—Europe—Guidebooks. 2. Europe—Guidebooks. I. Hotels
(Newton, Mass.)   II. Title.
TX907.5.E85B58   1994
647.94401--dc20   93–49499
                                              CIP

CAVEAT– Information in this text is believed accurate, and will pose no problem for the student or casual reader.
However, the author was often constrained by information contained in signed release forms, information that could have
been in error or not included at all. Any misinformation (or lack of information) is the result of failure in these attestations.
The author has done whatever is possible to insure accuracy.

Color separation, printing and binding by
Toppan Printing Co. (H.K.) Ltd. Hong Kong

10 9 8 7 6 5 4 3 2 1

Printed in China

This book is dedicated to Michelle Rodgers
whose love of travel and passion for Europe is infectious.
And to George Rodgers for supporting her indulgence.

W.B.

CONTENTS

FOREWORD

———— ❦ ————

As an associate editor of *Town & Country* magazine and a granddaughter of William Randolph Hearst, I feel qualified to discuss anything that is either historical, hysterical or just plain out of the ordinary.

Historically, this book has a lot to offer. There are several hotels with a dubious past. The Château de Bellinglise in France was once used to imprison Joan of Arc, and in England the Hartwell House was the home of King Louis XVIII, the exiled King of France.

Hysterically speaking, the Stone Age-style architecture of the Hotel Pitrizza in Sardinia and the cylindrical water tower turned respite in Germany are the most amusing. Everything else is wonderfully out of the ordinary.

This book is perfect for us sojourners whose travels keep us wandering nomadically through Europe. How wonderful to know that besides the typical hostelries it is possible to stay in a converted monastery in Portofino, a summer palace in Vienna, or a 900-year-old King Arthur-like castle in England.

Europe itself is so steeped in culture it is truly a living museum. An escape to European grandeur surrounded by friezes, frescoes and important picture galleries is a tremendous luxury. After an exhilarating day visiting cultural sites, who would not long to return to an antique-filled boudoir and collapse on an enormous canopy bed...or dine beneath vaulted ceilings heavy with frescoes...or read poetry in a scented garden designed by Capability Brown? It would be difficult not to get caught up in the fantasy of being part of another time—halcyon days when knights fought dragons, kings pursued handmaidens and ladies swooned.

This book is much more than a collection of unique and elegant European hotels...*it's a door into another world.*

Anne Randolph Hearst
Associate Editor, *Town & Country* magazine

PREFACE

〜❧〜

A s the publisher of an international business magazine for owners and managers of hotels, we initially questioned whether there would be sufficient interest in a top quality design book specifically focused on hotels. After all, the number of hotels that are designed or remodeled in a given year is quite small compared to the number of office buildings, houses, shopping centers or virtually any other type of building. Also, many hotels are of hotel chain "cookie-cutter" design, further reducing the number of unique hotel designs.

Was there really a market for a book on hotel design? PBC International, a publisher specializing in design books, came to us four years ago with the idea of doing a hotel design book. We agreed that the concept was intriguing, and our first book sold out in less than a year. Our next book is now in its second printing. Our third book sold out in less than a year and now we are proud to introduce this, our fourth hotel design book. *Elegant Hotels of Europe* was published not only for designers and hoteliers but for active and armchair travelers, too. In it we feature small hotels (under one hundred rooms) in Europe that are of unique design and style. Many of the properties included feature centuries-old architecture and regional design.

Apart from the high quality of the books, we believe that the immense popularity of this series is due to innate interest by designers and consumers alike in hotels. Tell an acquaintance that you have just returned from another city and invariably the first question will be "Where did you stay?" Of all buildings, hotels provide the complete array of human life experiences including environmental, dining, sleeping, entertainment, exercise, recreation, and through meetings and conventions, a work environment and educational experience.

Because the hotel provides a complete range of challenges and opportunities for its designers, a book on hotel design provides a wealth of ideas that readers can refine and adapt to their own requirements.

In addition to design, this book provides its readers with an interesting array of small, wonderful hotels to visit someday. For now, we hope that you enjoy your travels through these pages.

Don Lock
Publisher, *HOTELS* magazine

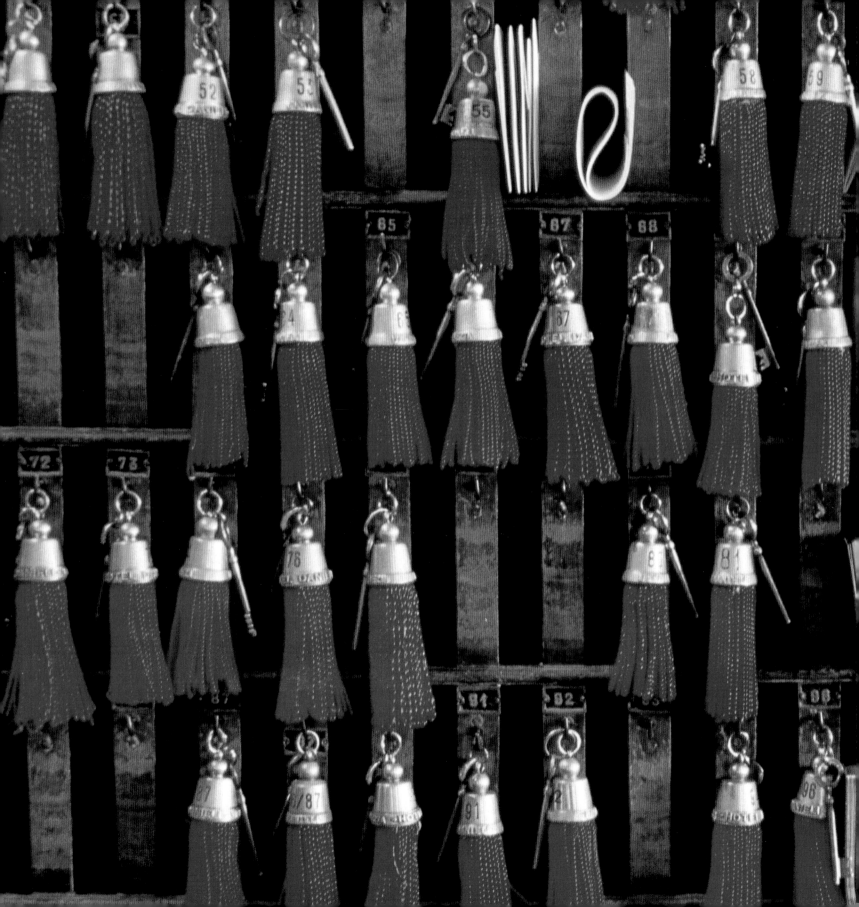

INTRODUCTION

Very few of life's experiences provide such luxurious gratification as a wonderful European hotel. I had always seen these luxury hotels as legendary places belonging to the storybook world. Eventually I was able to reside in my fantasies, and the dreams became reality. At first I felt more comfortable in the large hotels with anonymous luxury and the services of a well-trained concierge. But once I left the venerable grands for the more charming and intimate experience, I have rarely wanted to return. These boutique hotels—each under one hundred rooms—are the hotels I want to visit over and over again.

There is a growing trend among travelers, both sophisticated and novice, to experience boutique hotels and intimate inns. Once they were difficult to find, but today these gems are becoming more prevalent and accessible. Because of the worldwide economic downturn, the grand manses and castles of the former aristocracy are no longer affordable within families. Rather than face bankruptcy or demolition, these historic properties are now being converted to enchanting inns, and what makes them so charming is that many of the conversions were lovingly accomplished by distant relatives of original owners. Many were converted by those who have a vested interest in maintaining the dignity and grandeur of the past, and sharing it with those who also want to experience the magic. Today these hotels are more accessible because of communication wizardry—even most of the smallest hotels have a fax machine.

The smaller European hotels have more soul. They have as much, if not more history than their larger cousins, and somehow their legends seem more real. Several hotels in this book possess a questionable past. Who really slept there? Among many of the converted castles, apparitions even make regular visits. Somehow these hotels have the ability to possess your memories.

Don't expect the traditional hotel trappings. In many properties, the front desk is gone. Instead, friends are invited for a cup of tea or champagne while registering their stay. And, while luxurious, many of these smaller properties possess a comfortable residential ambiance—something today's larger hotels continually strive to achieve. In these boutique hotels the art is real and the accessories movable, while the eclectic decor truly conveys old-world charm.

The Continent has always been a romantic travel destination: the history, the customs, the people, the architecture, the food, the style. To me, Europe represents the essence of the romantic travel experience. Whether a sophisticated sojourner or an armchair enthusiast, I hope you will enjoy traveling through the pages of this book. These hotels don't necessarily represent the best that Europe has to offer, but rather a sampling of favorites. The back of the book contains a section called "Hotel Amenities." Here you can find out how to book a room at one of these wonderful properties, the *Elegant Hotels of Europe*.

W.B.

URBAN RETREATS

CHAPTER I

Located on the banks of the Grand Canal, this fifteenth-century palace once belonged to the Doge Andrea Gritti.

Outdoor dining at the Gritti Palace provides fabulous views of the ancient city of Venice.

The elegance of The Gritti Palace is evident in every corner of this architectural treasure.

Venice, Italy

HOTEL GRITTI PALACE

Designed as the castle of a noble Venetian family, the magnificent Hotel Gritti Palace is a historical reference to the elegance and romance of Venice. According to Ernest Hemingway in "Across the River into the Trees," the Gritti Palace is "the best hotel in a city of great hotels." The same judgment was echoed by Horace Sutton in his well-known travel book, *Footloose in Italy.*

Located on the banks of the Grand Canal, this fifteenth-century palace once belonged to the Doge Andrea Gritti. The architecture of the old house is undeniably Byzantine with Romanesque and Gothic influences. The Venetian styling of the time was incorporated as well—evident in the crenelated walls, in the tracery of the mullioned windows, in the porticos and in the open stairways leading to courtyards with parapets surrounding wells.

The Gritti became a hotel as an annex of the Grand Hotel, which was considered the most luxurious in Venice. The two properties were linked by a covered bridge. The Gritti was used for more sophisticated and eminent guests. This is how it was when Ciga found it and reopened it in June of 1948. It rapidly became known as one of Europe's celebrated destinations, frequented by the royal and the rich. The Gritti is purposely small, at only ninety-five rooms, yet includes every possible luxury and superb accommodations with personal attention for a limited number of privileged guests.

The Gritti Palace is celebrated for its art and artifacts including the Murano crystal wall sconces containing pure gold.

In 1987, a partial renovation took place by architect Maurizio Papire, whose choice for a five-shade basic color scheme included green, pale blue, pink, ivory and wood following the traditional tonal range of Venetian interiors of the past. Each of nineteen renovated "Gritti" rooms were painstakingly crafted, including the hand-painted decorative work, the cornices and carvings and the gold and silver leafing. Exquisite craftsmanship is also evident in the handmade mirrors by the master glass makers of Murano who were also responsible for the classic eighteenth-century style wall lights with crystal drops containing pure gold. Such opulence is evident, too, in the damask used for the curtains, the bed drapes and the wall hangings—all of the purest silk and woven by the longest established textile manufacturer in Venice. The overall effect of the interiors has been likened to that of an eighteenth-century music box.

Each of the Gritti bedrooms
is unique in its grandeur
and craftsmanship.

Designed as the castle
of a noble Venetian
family, the magnificent
Hotel Gritti Palace is a
historical reference
to the elegance and
romance of Venice.

The Hotel Gritti Palace
includes every possible
luxury and superb
accommodations for a
limited number of
privileged guests.

The gastronomic delights of
the Gritti Restaurant can
only be surpassed by the
decor of the elegant
dining room.

A section of the painting *Vienna, View from Belvedere* by Caneletto hangs in the Kunsthistoriche Museum and illustrates what the gardens must have looked like.

ALI MEYER, FINE ARTS PHOTOGRAPHY

HOTEL IM PALAIS SCHWARZENBERG

Built between 1697 and 1727 by the famous masters of baroque Lukas von Hildebrandt and Fischer von Erlach, the Palais Schwarzenberg has remained the Vienna summer residence of the Schwarzenberg family. The family was known for their substantial land holdings, their social stature and their commitment as patrons of the arts. Both Hayden and Beethoven, among others, gave first performances of some of their work at the Palais Schwarzenberg. For more than two centuries, the Palais remained one of the important meeting points in the imperial capital for the world of arts, politics, literature and society—but on a strictly private basis.

This historical palace has been available to the public as a thirty-eight room hotel since the mid-1960s. Located in the center of Vienna, the property is surrounded by 18 acres of private park and gardens. The Marmorsaal (Marble Hall) and the Kuppelsaal (Entrance Hall) contain magnificent ceiling frescoes done from 1723 to 1724 by Daniel Gran who was considered one of Vienna's most famous baroque painters. A unique feature of this extremely elegant room is the baroque picture gallery where various

The Hotel im Palais Schwarzenberg is set on 18 acres of private parkland.

masterworks of different painters and schools are assembled into large square panels forming one large picture. Various other rooms contain substantial works by Peter Paul Rubens (*Ganymed* and *Romulus and Remus*). There is also a collection of still lifes by Franz Werner Tamm and a set of early seventeenth-century Meissen vases.

Because of the historic and artistic importance of the building and large parts of its interior, most of the public rooms are classified cultural heritage by the Austrian government. A visit to the Palais is a museum study in itself. In addition to the spectacular public spaces, each of the thirty-eight guest rooms are individually decorated mainly with Italian fabrics, period furniture and valuable paintings and etchings.

The thirty-eight bedrooms of the Palais are uniquely decorated with Italian fabrics, period furniture and valuable paintings and etchings.

The magnificent frescoes of the Marble Hall have remained virtually unaffected through the years.

The 125-year-old Amstel reopened in 1992 after extensive renovation.

Amsterdam, The Netherlands

AMSTEL HOTEL INTER·CONTINENTAL

The guest rooms feature rich, majestic colors combined with antique furniture, paintings and objets d'art.

The Amstel Hotel was once a jewel among European luxury hotels, but through the years the grande dame began to tarnish. Today, after a multi-million dollar face lift, the venerable hotel is once again serving five-star luxury for luminaries and well-heeled travelers.

Dutch architect Cornelius Outhsoorm saw the opulence and luxury of Amsterdam's royal buildings as inspiration for designing the Amstel in 1866. Given its regal surroundings, the architecture of the palatial building bore classical proportions and intricate interior detailing. The exterior is designed in the traditional Dutch/Victorian style, with distinctive patterned brickwork, timber-framed windows and gables. The exquisite architecture, together with the elegant surroundings quickly made the hotel the social center of the city.

Throughout the years, various additions and remodelings were done to the property. In 1990 it was determined that the wood pilings on which the hotel was built were beginning to retreat slowly into the banks of the Amstel River. The hotel was closed for two years for complete renovation. Architectural firm RTKL took care to preserve the historically registered Grand Hall and upper mezzanine, grand sweeping staircase, the Mirror Room and the Sarphati and Stadhouders Rooms. The former 111 guest rooms were converted into seventy-nine luxurious spaces and the exterior brick, timber and stone façade was cleaned and preserved. The hotel reopened in 1992.

AMSTEL
INTER·CONTINENTAL
AMSTERDAM

The exterior is designed
in the traditional
Dutch/Victorian style, with
distinctive patterned
brickwork, timber-framed
windows and gables.

The skillful refurbishment
has re-created the
atmosphere that once
delighted the nineteenth-
century traveler.

From the grandeur of the reception area, to the overall warm, intimate atmosphere, nothing has been overlooked.

The exquisite architecture, together with the elegant surroundings quickly made the hotel the social center of the city.

The new indoor pool has elegant columns and marbled floors.

French designer Pierre Yves Rochon was chosen to create the interiors with the achieved goal of producing the feeling of the country residence of a European nobleman. Two basic colors, china blue and terracotta, were chosen for the bedrooms, and many of the bedspreads and wall coverings used toile de Jouy designs. Locally commissioned objets d'art such as carriage clocks, plates and vases were used to create a homey feel. Most of the antique furnishings were salvaged from the former interiors.

STUDIO BRACKFROCK GMBH, HAMBURG, GERMANY

Architecturally, the
Goldener Hirsch features
thick plaster walls and
archways, and numerous
rooms with vaulted ceilings.

STUDIO BRACKFROCK GMBH, HAMBURG, GERMANY

In the very heart of ancient Salzburg stands the venerable Hotel Goldener Hirsch, one of Europe's main cultural and meeting locations. The name of this inn means "golden stag" and even today the magnificent collection of baroque antlers reflects the old hunting lodge feeling the hotel has known since its first mention in 1407. This historic hotel sits just a few doors down from the birthplace of Salzburg's most famous son, Mozart. But even at the time of Mozart's birth in 1756, the Goldener Hirsch was already a famous "gasthous" (inn).

Almost six hundred years of European culture can be seen in the architecture and furnishings of the Goldener Hirsch, including provincial furniture, antique paintings, hand-blocked textiles and many lovingly chosen antique accessories which create an atmosphere reflecting the charm of its patrician past. Each of the seventy-three guest rooms of the main house feature rustic Austrian antique pieces and renaissance locks. In 1987 the hotel acquired the fourteenth-century Kupferschmiedhaus (former home to the copper smithy) across the street which consists of seventeen double rooms, each individually decorated in local Salzburg style.

Architecturally, the hotel features thick plaster walls and archways and numerous rooms with vaulted ceilings. Several of the arched windows feature antique glass reminiscent of ancient glass bottles.

Salzburg, Austria

HOTEL GOLDENER HIRSCH

STUDIO BRACKFROCK GMBH, HAMBURG, GERMANY

A few doors away from the
birthplace of Mozart is the
Hotel Goldener Hirsch.
The hotel's name means
"golden stag."

Guest rooms and suites
preserve the romantic
charm of a
fifteenth-century inn.

This ornate bed and armoire
are some of the carefully
selected antique
furnishings in the hotel.

The hotel's original brick structure served as Europe's tallest water tower.

The contrast of pillars and modern walkways creates an interplay between contemporary functionality and historic authenticity.

Many styles claim to blend the old with the new, but such is truly the case in the design of the Hotel im Wasserturm in Cologne. Formerly Europe's tallest water tower, this cylindrical structure was built in 1872 by British engineer John Moore to serve the needs of the local community. When the city rapidly outgrew the water tower's capacity, an underground piping system was installed. The structure succumbed to use as a workshop and warehouse.

It wasn't until 1985 that its future use as a luxury hotel would be realized. The architectural task of K.L. Heinrichs was to retain the monumental, strictly tectonic shape of the tower and not limit its original effect in any way—as stipulated by the regional and city conservation authorities. At the same time, however, it was necessary to create windows for lighting as the existing were only blind arches and blind windows. The tower was heightened to its pre-war scale with bricks fired in the original color, consistency and dimensions.

Another challenge to this unique project was to provide interiors that could be compatible as well as in contrast to the unique structure. French designer Andrée Putman was chosen to provide a mixture of luxury and timeless classicism. Materials such as "shot glass," dark African woods and corroded metal harmonized well with the original brickwork. The color range includes toned shades of beige and brown in combination with accents of yellow and blue. The diamond and cylindrical shapes of the tower are repeated throughout the contemporary interiors. Every piece of furniture and each accessory within the ninety-bedroom hotel has been designed by Putman. The hotel also features more than 350 original paintings by contemporary artists.

The experience of this unique luxury hotel has been available to guests since 1990. It is the combination of remarkable design and restrained elegance that will distinguish the Hotel im Wasserturm well into the future.

Cologne, Germany

HOTEL IM WASSERTURM

The cylindrical motif of the hotel is played upon in its interior design.

French designer Andrée Putman was chosen to provide a mixture of luxury and timeless classicism to the interiors of the Hotel im Wasserturm.

The building's complex architecture created unique bedrooms made interesting through contemporary furnishings.

The Hotel im Wasserturm is elegant throughout, even in its beautiful and spacious bathrooms.

Le Richemond began as a twenty-five room boarding house known as the Riche-Mont Pension.

Le Richemond is both elegant and efficient, providing modern amenities in complete luxury.

Geneva, Switzerland

LE RICHEMOND

In Switzerland, the hotel industry is considered an extremely noble and important profession. In fact, the Swiss have set the standard for innkeeping and service, as the famous hotel school in Lausanne continues. But even Grand Hotels are not made overnight. It has taken 118 years and four generations of the same family to produce this hotel gem.

With only ninety-nine guest rooms, Le Richemond is not considered a large hotel, but its reputation is vast. According to the fourth generation leadership of the hotel, a Grand Hotel must combine the three basic ingredients of art, culture and professional management. Judged by these criteria, the Armleder family seem to be born hoteliers. They consider it their birthright to continue the tradition as Grand hoteliers to lend Le Richemond the exclusiveness of a private club and the glamour of theater, together with just a hint of off-stage mystery. Add to that the quest for perfection and absolutely impeccable service and you have the art of the hotel.

In 1875, what began as a twenty-five-room boarding house known as the Riche-Mont Pension provided the setting for the future of the Armleders—a family well known in Switzerland for their leadership in the art of the hotel. Today Le Richemond is both elegant and efficient and provides such unique features as a refrigerated caviar trolley, generations of collected art and antiques, and detailed architecture and interiors. The public spaces are paved in rich carpets while the walls and ceilings glisten with highly polished and carved wood. The hotel is furnished with traditional pieces of various styles—each guest room unique. Interior styles range from Louis XV and Louis XVI to Empire and Napoleon III while the exterior has a vaguely art deco façade. The location is perfect, alongside of Lake Geneva with a fantastic view of the Alps and, in particular, Mont Blanc.

The public spaces are
paved in rich carpets while
the walls and ceilings
glisten with highly polished
and carved wood.

The rich interiors of the
Suite Colette.

35

Salzburg's Radisson Hotel Altstadt traces its origins to three houses built between 1290 and 1693.

Located in the heart of Salzburg's "Old Town," the sixty-two-room Altstadt is one of the premier boutique hotels in Europe.

Salzburg, Austria

RADISSON HOTEL ALTSTADT

Some of the guest rooms feature the ancient exposed beams and stucco ceilings of Austrian heritage.

Salzburg's Radisson Hotel Altstadt traces its origins to three houses built between 1290 and 1693. Located in the heart of Salzburg's "Old Town," this sixty-two-room luxury hotel is today one of the premier boutique hotels in Europe.

Documents show that the name Brauhaus (Brew House) first appears as a description of the house in 1451. It served as such until 1922 when beer brewing became unprofitable. Several major renovations were undertaken, including one in 1992 which was a historically correct architectural renovation completed to preserve the property.

From the moment one enters this 500-year-old building, one can feel the unique atmosphere. Untersberger marble alternates with rough-hewn stone. Select antiques blend perfectly with classically elegant furnishings, and fine paintings grace the walls. Some of the low ceilings and stone archways are indicative of the ancient architecture. Older features of the hotel can be seen in the Altdeutsches Zimmer (Old German Lounge) with its dark wood paneling, rustic decor and stained glass windows. Among new architectural features is a glass-roofed atrium which can be seen from each floor. Overall, the feeling is of old-world elegance.

No two rooms of the hotel are alike—an unusual feature for an American hotel chain. Each was renovated and furnished with attention to detail. Some feature the ancient exposed beams and elegant stucco ceilings of Austrian heritage. In all cases, the rooms feature the charm of this historical hotel.

Views of the historic city of
Salzburg unfold through the
restaurant's windows.

Each room was renovated
and furnished with special
attention to detail.

A historically correct
renovation was undertaken
in 1992 to preserve
the property.

Each lovingly restored
detail contributes to
the atmosphere of
this enchanting and
historic hotel.

In contrast to its
traditional exterior and
historic environs,
the inside of The Halkin
is stylishly modern.

The newly constructed hotel
was designed to fit into
the elegant
Belgravia neighborhood.

London, England

THE HALKIN

In a city dominated by old traditional town house hotels, the newly constructed Halkin stands out. Situated in the fashionable Belgravia area, the five-story, forty-one-room hotel features an elegant façade of dark brick combined with Portland stone and a copper roof.

In contrast to its traditional exterior and historic environs, the inside of The Halkin is stylishly modern, but possesses a sense of elegance and comfort. Terrazzo and mosaic marble on the floors, wood veneers and encaustic plaster give The Halkin an Italian theme. Comfortable sofas, bright blue leather bucket chairs and casual draping on the windows give the lounge a chic look.

The decor in the rooms is striking. Though each room is uniquely decorated with eclectic style, each of the five floors are color coordinated to comply with the five elements: water, air, fire, earth and sky. The suites, rooms and public areas are finished to the highest visual standard featuring exotic hardwoods, leather, marble and silk. Oriental antiques are offset by halogen lighting. Marble and glass, and elegant fixtures make the bathrooms impressive throughout.

The atmosphere at The Halkin is unique in London. Its original, clean design will appeal to travelers with a preference for private luxury, contemporary design, quiet and a minimum of fuss.

The atmosphere at
The Halkin is unique
in London. Its original,
clean design will appeal
to travelers with a
preference for private
luxury, contemporary
design, quiet and a
minimum of fuss.

Bathrooms are large and feature extensive use of marble and glass.

The reception hall is sleek and paved with marble.

The suites, rooms and public areas are finished to the highest visual standard.

TOWN HOUSE HOTELS

CHAPTER II

Behind the Corinthian columns of the portal lie the luxurious comforts of 47 Park Street.

The drawing room features warm oak paneling and an Anglo-French chic style.

London, England

47 PARK STREET

First appearances can be deceiving, and in the case of the luxury hotel 47 Park Street, this is certainly true. Located in the fashionable London Mayfair neighborhood, this fifty-two-suite hotel is an intimate and discreet establishment, concealed behind a typical neighborhood Edwardian façade.

Historically, the land was a cultivated pasture area owned by London's largest landowner—His Grace, the Duke of Westminster. The property wasn't developed until 1926, when the first Baron Milford built exclusive *pied à terre* apartments for country gentlemen visiting London. In 1981, Albert Roux moved his already famous restaurant, La Gavroche, to the premises. The elegant hotel was designed as a natural extension of the renowned restaurant.

Once through the discreet front of 47 Park Street, guests enter an atmosphere of Anglo-French chic created by Monique Roux. The foyer, with its light oak paneling, leads into a paneled drawing room, lined with books and decorated with original oil paintings and ornaments. Scatter cushions in subtle hues rest on sofas and chairs furnished in the best traditional British fabrics. Each of the fifty-two suites are infused with Madame Roux's inimitable sense of relaxed French style—no two rooms alike. Each room is furnished with natural fabrics, yew on limed oak furniture, and paintings and accessories discovered over the years in England.

Many of the original architectural features remain today, including a beautiful curved iron staircase and a series of striking art nouveau style stained glass windows. Giant Corinthian columns are built into the wings at either end of the façade facing Park Street. All the guest rooms feature a separate in-room dining area, a large drawing room and a fully equipped kitchen.

A striking iron staircase and art nouveau style stained glass windows remain from the hotel's original structure.

The spacious bedrooms feature the best of French design and British fabrics.

The Lancaster's elegance maintains its reputation as a favorite of royalty, society and leading figures of government and the arts.

RIGHT
French ottoman curtain fabric of soft stripes was chosen for the French windows that overlook the courtyard in the foyer. These curtains were lined with a Colefax & Fowler fabric, which provides an equally pretty view back into the foyer.

O ne of France's best kept secrets lies hidden among the busiest and most vulgar of Parisian boulevards. It is so well disguised that even today taxicabs and passersby easily miss the discreet green awning of The Lancaster's façade—unless, of course, they are destined to be there. The lovely Lancaster is one of Europe's most charming hotels, with an undisputed reputation for impeccable standards and service.

The Lancaster was built in 1889 as a private belle epoque town house. It remained that way until 1925 when it was sold to Swiss hotelier Emile Wolf.

Paris, France
THE LANCASTER

Known for referring to all his patrons as "friends" rather than guests, Wolf transformed the building into eight floors of hotel.

Wolf was set on retaining the original architectural features and much of the furniture during his sensitive transformation. The conversion was completed in 1930 with the aid of Wolf's housekeeper, the daughter of an antique dealer. Together they established the hotel's character which has been described as rather like an eighteenth-century antique and art show. Remaining evidence of Wolf's style includes Barye bronzes, rows of kakiemon vases and Louis XV and Louis XVI style furniture.

LEFT
Opulent murals and rich wood furnishings make the Lancaster Bar a perfect rendezvous spot in the center of Paris.

Most of the furniture pieces are good nineteenth-century copies.

Recently The Lancaster's eighteenth-century interior was renovated under the careful direction of the general manager, M. Francois Touzin. Each of the sixty-six rooms, the front hall and the foyer were renovated under the supervision of Prue Lane-Fox. French ottoman curtain fabric of soft stripes was chosen for the French windows that overlook the courtyard in the foyer. The curtains were ingeniously lined with a Colefax & Fowler fabric to ensure that guests dining in the summertime courtyard have an equally pretty view back into the foyer. Comfortable cane sofas were covered with red cotton damask and a chevron pattern was used on the chairs. The rooms, a tasteful study in walnut and brocade were restored to their best. Each bathroom features beautifully maintained art deco fittings and tiles.

Today, The Lancaster continues to be operated as it always has—as a luxurious, private home, filled with a fascinating collection of furniture, candelabra, paintings, chandeliers, lamps, tapestries, velvets, silk and damask, crystal and porcelain. With its sixty-six individually styled rooms, romantic courtyard restaurant and elegant public areas, The Lancaster remains a favorite of royalty, society and leading figures of government and the arts. The Lanc, as it is affectionately known, has received such famous "friends" as Greta Garbo, Joseph Kennedy, Noel Coward, Clark Gable, Sir Alec Guiness, John Huston, Gregory Peck, John Steinbeck and Steven Spielberg.

Bedrooms include eighteenth-century works of art, Persian rugs and porcelain.

Each bathroom features beautifully maintained art deco fittings and tiles.

The lovely Lancaster is one of Europe's most charming hotels, with an undisputed reputation for impeccable standards and service.

The courtyard's bronze bust of Minerva and pair of gilded art deco bronze fawns by Pompon were received as payment for a hotel bill.

The welcoming facade of Paris's fashionable Hôtel San Regis.

Paris, France

HÔTEL SAN REGIS

With the trend moving away from large, well-known hotels, a fashionable boutique hotel such as Paris's Hôtel San Regis may be the perfect place to stay. This forty-four-room hotel not only offers guests the residential home-away-from-home feel that weary travelers seek, but does so in a great location. Visitors are only a five-minute walk to the Christian Dior boutique, Restaurant Lasserre or the Théâtre des Champs-Elysées, as the hotel is situated near the Avenue Montaigne, the Champs-Elysées and the Faubourg St-Honoré.

This stylish hotel was originally constructed in 1857 as a private house which included an entresol, a ground floor, two main floors and an annex for servants and horses. The location was perfect even then for Sunday excursions up the Champs-Elysées in the family barouche. Somewhere around the turn of the century, the property was purchased by Mr. Simon-Andre Terrail (father of Claude Terrail, present owner of the famous restaurant La Tour d'Argent) to house foreign visitors. By 1930, the top floor was demolished and replaced with five additional floors which are included in the current seven-floor hotel. In 1984, the San Regis was completely remodeled into what is now one of the more elegant, yet comfortable hotels in Paris. The winter garden was also created at this time to bring light to the dining room and bar. The lounge was fitted with beautifully carved wood-panel walls, nineteenth-century antiques and comfortable upholstered furniture.

Each bedroom in this cozy urban retreat is unique, featuring distinct colors, design and period antiques—mostly Louis XV, Louis XVI and Empire. All rooms are very tastefully appointed with wallpaper, artwork and comfortable upholstery. Some of the rooms feature duplex suites with circular stairs.

At this exclusive Parisian boutique hotel, one need only walk out the door to be a part of the romantic City of Lights, or enjoy the city's view from atop the terrace.

This forty-four-room hotel not only offers guests the residential home-away-from-home feel that weary travelers seek, but does so in a great location.

Each bedroom is unique, featuring distinct colors, designs and period antiques.

In 1984, the
Hôtel San Regis was
remodeled into what is now
one of the more elegant,
yet comfortable hotels in
Paris. The winter garden
was created at this time to
bring light into the
dining room and bar.

The surroundings of
the lounge feature antique
wood paneling,
period antique furniture
and comfortable
upholstered pieces.

All the rooms are very
tastefully appointed with
wallpaper, artwork and
comfortable upholstery.

BOB ANTON

© ARCADIA

© ARCADIA / FABRICE RAMBERT

The country house style of The Beaufort makes for a homey, comfortable stay in this private hotel.

Pink and green sofas, chintz cushions and curtains, and bleached wood side tables give the drawing room a residential feel.

London, England

THE BEAUFORT

Positioned 100 yards from Harrods in a tree-lined square, the twenty-eight-room Beaufort hotel is perfectly situated for shopping, business and experiencing London. There is no formal reception desk. Upon arrival, guests need only sign the guest book at which time they are given a front door key and shown to their rooms. It is then that not only the warmth and coziness of this hotel become evident, but also the commitment to comfortable service and security.

The hotel was purchased in 1986 by Diana Wallis who had traveled extensively and knew what she wanted from an architectural, design and service standpoint. She immediately set to the task of remodeling and decorating the two tall early Victorian town houses. Today, guests may lounge in the drawing room with its oversized sofas, chairs, magazine covered tables, flower arrangements and delicate trompe l'oeil arches against a blue-washed background.

Wallis has decorated each of the twenty-eight bedrooms uniquely, using only those materials she would be happy to use in her own home. The English country house style includes walls hung with pale marbled papers; fabrics by Baker's and Parkertex, and Osborne and Little in pastoral designs with flowers, trees and birds; and wool carpets that are deep and warm cream in color. More than three hundred original English watercolors don the walls. In addition to the comfortable residential atmosphere, the Beaufort guest rooms feature decanters of brandy, Swiss chocolates, fruit, shortbread and flowers everywhere. Wallis adamantly refused to use heavy contract furniture or "nail down" any of the room accessories.

Impeccable and discreet service is a primary concern and all extras are included in the price. Tipping is discouraged. This privately-owned town house hotel has been designated among the best in the world by several travel guides.

In addition to the
comfortable residential
atmosphere, The Beaufort's
guest rooms feature
decanters of brandy,
Swiss chocolates, fruit,
shortbread, and
flowers everywhere.

KEN KIRKWOOD

57

Les Etoiles's panoramic view
is unparalleled in Rome.

Rome, Italy

ATLANTE STAR

If location is everything, then the Atlante Star in Rome is the place to be. The hotel itself is just a few steps from St. Peter's Basilica and Vatican City.

The building was originally an apartment Palazzetto built at the end of the 1800s, and the hotel's exterior architecture still features some of the original floral decorations. Today, the eighty-room hotel features a tastefully renovated lobby covered with dark marble, chrome trim and wood. The upper floors and guest rooms evoke a feeling of being aboard a luxuriously appointed ocean liner. The rooms feature the lavish use of curved and lacquered surfaces and furniture, and extensive use of ubatuba granite. The walls are upholstered in fresh printed fabrics and silk wall tapestry.

Each room features modern bathrooms and carpeting, and art deco inspired door handles and fittings. The two conference rooms are very well appointed for any executive function.

Situated on the rooftop of the Atlante Star, the Les Etoiles restaurant features a garden and is known for its superior, traditional and creative cuisine. This restaurant features a symphony of flavors surrounded by elegance. At the Les Etoiles one can experience a 360-degree panorama of the entire city, which includes a view of Michelangelo's Dome. The view alone is worth the visit on a warm Roman night when the dome of St. Peter's is illuminated and the crenelated walls of Castle Sant' Angelo brood over the Tiber.

The conference rooms feature everything a discriminating executive could desire.

A suite at the Atlante Star has all the modern comforts.

This beautiful belle epoque town house is located off the world-famous Champs-Elysées.

Terrace dining at Hôtel Balzac's famous address provides a panoramic view of the City of Lights.

Paris, France

THE HÔTEL BALZAC

The Hôtel Balzac originated in 1910 as a belle epoque town house on the street of the famous nineteenth-century French writer Honoré de Balzac. It remained the residence of an aristocratic Parisian family until 1985. It was then that the new owner appointed Serge Brunst, an interior designer with an appreciation for antiques and travel who attended the Beaux Arts School in Paris, to take on The Hôtel Balzac as his first hotel project.

The owner's aim was to create an intimate and charming atmosphere within this prime Parisian location—just off the Champs-Elysées. During the renovation of this seventy-room hotel, the main architectural structures, the inner patio and the elegant belle epoque façade were left intact. The patio's roof has been enhanced by a glass ceiling. The new decor subtly blends traditional architecture with comfortable but modern amenities. The public spaces are paved in imported marble. Light wood accents the guest rooms, which were redecorated in 1991. The reception area greets visitors with an eclectic array of fine oil paintings, antique tapestries and oriental rugs. Just outside, the historic façade is punctuated with scarlet shades and traditional geraniums.

In September 1990, the internationally known restaurant Bicé, designed by New Yorker Adam Tihany, opened its Parisian doors at the Hôtel Balzac. From its mahogany and sycamore-paneled interiors to the engraved mirrors and 1930s fixtures, this popular restaurant combines its art deco atmosphere well with the traditional elegance of the hotel. The Hôtel Balzac is recognized as one of Paris's most intimate and charming luxury hotels.

The elegantly appointed
lobby is paved in imported
marble and features
exquisite art and antiques.

The Hôtel Balzac is
recognized as one of Paris's
most intimate and charming
luxury hotels.

Each room is
beautifully designed
and furnished.

Dukes Hotel was
established in 1908, but
the main building dates to
1895 and is full of
historical references.

London, England

DUKES HOTEL

Dukes Hotel is situated in a flower-filled courtyard in London's Saint James Square. Known as one of London's most charming hotels, this property offers all modern amenities, while still retaining the elegance of a beautifully preserved Edwardian building.

Dukes was established as a hotel in 1908, but the main building dates back to 1895 and is full of historical references. The courtyard around which Dukes stands led to the house of Barbara Villiers, Dutchess of Cleveland, one of King Charles II's mistresses. The building that is today Dukes Hotel was originally used as London chambers for the sons of nobility. The location, St. James Place, has been home to many famous writers, musicians, bankers and politicians. Sir Edward Elgar, the famous British composer, lived at Dukes Hotel when in the city for concerts.

One of the nicest attractions about this sixty-four-room hotel is its feeling of secluded intimacy. The furnishings are rich in English heritage featuring fine classic antiques and marble bathrooms. Each of the rooms are individually designed and furnished. Of the rooms, twenty-six are luxurious suites featuring separate bedroom, sitting room and kitchenette. The hotel also features a terrace providing spectacular views across the rooftops of London.

COUNTRY INNS

CHAPTER III

The severe stone façade of Ston Easton Park contrasts with the ornate eighteenth-century interior architecture.

The Saloon is renowned for its eighteenth-century reliefs, Corinthian columns and magnificent plaster ceiling.

Someone once said, "The single greatest contribution of the English to the art of living is the English country house." One of the finest examples of this style lies near the cities of Bath and Bristol in the peaceful village of Ston Easton. The historical Palladian mansion of Ston Easton Park, as seen today, was built in 1740 and features some of the finest architectural interior decoration in the west of England. The house is set in a romantic, classic landscape created by Humphry Repton, noted designer of the eighteenth century. The River Norr flows through the gardens.

When the house was purchased in the 1960s by the Smedley family, it was in grave disrepair and had been granted a demolition order. The family purchased the property and intended to keep it as a private home, gradually restoring it over the years. However, the high cost of the lengthy refurbishment convinced them to make just seven of the bedrooms available to the public in 1982. Within a few months of opening, the hostelry was awarded the coveted "Hotel of the Year." This encouraged them to retain the services of interior designer Jean Monro, respected as one of the great authorities in Britain on eighteenth-century interiors, to help design the rest of the hotel and the conversion of twenty-two bedrooms.

Somerset, England

STON EASTON PARK

Elaborate architectural
detailing and trompe l'oeil
wall-covering provide a
dramatic backdrop for
fine furnishings in the
Print Room.

Some of the bedrooms have original Chippendale four-poster beds, Fortuny fabrics, needlepoint chairs and William and Mary marquetry chests.

Very little of the previous structure exists today, however one internal wall still incorporates the stone-mullioned windows and wood paneling of Jacobean times. The exterior façade of this now famous hotel is rather severe and symmetrical with its plaster and dressed stone. By contrast, however, the interior architecture is elaborate eighteenth-century and magnificently portrayed throughout the house. The Entrance Hall features a coved ceiling and is notable for the quality of its plaster work. The lintels are elaborately carved and an eighteenth-century lantern hangs from the ceiling.

The Saloon has been described as the finest room in Somerset. On either side of the main door and above the fireplace are grisaille paintings on canvas simulating the stone reliefs of the eighteenth century while the main door is flanked by elaborate Corinthian columns and a pediment of magnificently carved wood. The Saloon's ceiling is unrivaled with its scene of an eagle and Jupiter descending from the sun. A frieze of shells and floral garlands encircles the walls.

The Victorian design of the building was conceived by architect Issac Barradale in the tradtional style of the "Old English."

Nina Campbell masterminded the renovation of Hambleton Hall, creating a haven of style and charm combined with complete comfort.

Rutland, England

HAMBLETON HALL

Hambleton Hall was built in 1881 as a traditional English "hunting box" when Rutland and its surroundings were considered the epitome for fox hunters from everywhere.

The Victorian design of the building was conceived by architect Isaac Barradale in the traditional style of the "Old English." The asymmetrical plan has made for a comfortable interior today. The house remained within the same family until 1979 when it was purchased to be converted into a luxurious country hotel. Nina Campbell, one of England's best-known interior designers, masterminded the renovation creating a haven of style and charm combined with complete comfort. Campbell's philosophy is to create a collection of fine furnishings, art and antiques while avoiding the catalog approach to decor. Each of the fifteen rooms and public spaces are uniquely appointed and create that special warmth of a fine personal residence. Campbell continues to supervise the redecoration year by year.

In 1976, the local area's landscape was altered by the creation of Rutland Waters, a reservoir for the local communities. It is because of this transformation that the hotel can provide a variety of additional activities, including some of the best fishing in Europe, sailing and windsurfing. The property still provides the traditional fox hunt as well as other shooting activities.

The glamour and luxury of the past are still present today as Hambleton Hall is considered among the best and most comfortable country house hotels outside London.

Each of the fifteen rooms and public spaces are uniquely appointed and create that special warmth of a fine personal residence.

A seat in the garden provides a relaxing resting place.

Hintlesham Hall's Tudor facade overlooks lush back lawns, the herb garden, pond, and an 18-hole championship golf course.

Set in the middle of 175 acres of rolling Suffolk countryside is one of England's premier country house hotels. Hintlesham Hall, hosting thirty-three bedrooms, architecturally spans 400 years while surprising visitors with several distinct styles. The famous Georgian façade might lead you to believe that the Hall had been built in the eighteenth century—that is, until you look up to see the unmistakably Elizabethan red chimney stacks. If you walk around to the rear, you will notice that the less well-known face of the Hall confirms its Tudor origins.

This conflict in styles represents the gracious heritage of this former manor house. The first recorded history of the manor dates to 1454 when a local family bought the home from a famous judge. In the 1570s, the entire property was rebuilt in the Elizabethan style of the day featuring a heavily timbered second floor and great red brick Tudor chimney stacks. Today this charming side of the hotel faces east overlooking lush back lawns, the herb garden, pond and an 18-hole championship golf course. The main side of the property contrasts with a stately Georgian façade, dating to 1720. The stucco, cornerstones and vertical sash windows display the formality of a different generation.

Suffolk, England

HINTLESHAM HALL

The interiors, too, represent an eclectic combination of styles. The Stuart period is represented by a splendid oak staircase leading to the north wing (carved by the famous seventeenth-century wood carver Grinling Gibbons) and the magnificent plaster work in the ceiling of the Carolean Room. Other major Georgian additions include not only the façade, but the pine paneling of the public rooms and the creation of the double height Salon with its delightful entrance arcade. The early nineties have seen the completion of a program of lavish refurbishment creating the thirty-three bedrooms and suites in different shapes, sizes and styles—some with four-poster or canopy beds. All the rooms are individually designed and furnished, each with a different character enhanced by elegant fabrics, antique furniture and works of art.

The Salon is the largest of three dining rooms.

The Library represents the combined elegance and comfort of Hintlesham Hall's public spaces.

Several of the bedrooms have heavily timbered walls and ceilings, antique furniture and comfortably coordinated fabrics.

The Lygon Arms is one of England's most celebrated coaching inns.

Only 90 miles from London lie the fairytale villages of the Cotswolds. With its great stone manors and thatched roof houses, this charming area of England has a style of its own. Set in the middle of the picturesque Cotswolds is the Lygon Arms, one of England's most celebrated sixteenth-century coaching inns.

This sixty-room inn is steeped in history. Throughout the property are reminders of a centuries-old civilization. During the Civil War, King Charles I conferred here with his confidants and Cromwell actually slept at the inn. The rooms named after them have retained many of their original features. Throughout the inn there are several period rooms filled with antiques, but the Lygon Arms also has more modern guest rooms in its Garden and Orchard wings.

The style of the restaurant is essentially English. As it is set in The Great Hall, guests of the restaurant can luxuriate by a roaring open fire under the seventeenth-century minstrel's gallery and heraldic friezes. In 1991 a new addition, known as the Country Club, was opened. Located adjacent to the hotel, the new building was sympathetically designed behind a mellow Cotswold stone façade to blend discreetly with the historic character of the old inn. Decorative wall tiles, murals and antiques, accentuated by trompe l'oeil, create a soothing environment for the pursuit of health and fitness.

One of the highlights of the hotel today comes from its historical refurbishment. At the turn of the century, S.B. Russell bought the magnificent but neglected inn. The expensive restoration meant that most of the profits were put back into the inn. The restoration of the furniture became so successful that visitors began requesting pieces. A small workshop, which son Gordon took charge of, was expanded to sell furniture. From the 1920s, Sir Gordon Russell furniture became part of the history of British design in the twentieth century.

Worcestershire, England

THE LYGON ARMS

The Garden and Orchard wings feature tastefully styled modern bedrooms that have received praise and commendation.

The Great Bedchamber features a romantic four-poster bed.

Blending well with the inn's 450 years of history and the style and courtesy of years gone by are the luxuries and comforts of today.

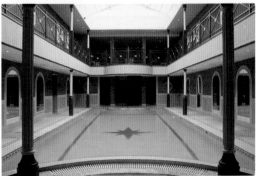

The ivy-covered brick façade of Chewton Glen belies its eighteenth-century beginnings.

Coordinated wall coverings and fabrics give this bedroom a cozy residential feel.

Rich Colefax and Fowler chintzes cover the luxurious bedrooms.

Hampshire, England

CHEWTON GLEN

Amid 70 acres of rolling parkland between the edge of the New Forest—once William the Conqueror's hunting grounds—and the English Channel sits Chewton Glen, widely regarded as the benchmark for British country house hotels.

It is the relentless commitment of proprietors Martin and Brigitte Skan to impeccable service and perfection that has created this storybook retreat. When the Skan family bought the hotel in 1966, it possessed eight drab bedrooms, one bathroom and a very leaky roof. Today the manor house includes sixty-two luxurious rooms—all with pristine white baths, a famous restaurant with a renowned wine list, a 9-hole golf course, putting green and a complete new health spa including state-of-the-art exercise equipment, Olympic-size pool and personal services.

Chewton Glen's architectural roots can be traced to records of a new classical Palladian-style country house built in the 1750s. Sometime in the 1830s a new curved central section in the "picturesque" style of that period was added. It wasn't until the early twentieth century that the façades were entirely remodeled in brick using the revived Queen Anne style.

The interiors are the creation of proprietress Brigitte Skan, an accomplished designer with an appropriate passion for Colefax and Fowler chintzes, and a determination that each room should have its own character. The elegant, yet cozy, hotel features extensive use of antique furnishings. The luxurious bathrooms have heated towel bars, telephones, bidets, double sinks set in marble and a multitude of mirrors. And, both the new health spa and conference rooms feature trompe l'oeil murals by English artist Chris Boulter depicting walls of warm golden faux stone set with shell-shaped niches and flower bearing urns, reminiscent of the old-world classical spas. Even the ceiling in the spa is floating with blue sky and fluffy clouds.

Middlethorpe Hall's garden front is an exercise in Queen Anne symmetry.

LUCINDA LAMBTON

The magnificent carved oak staircase in the stone-flagged entrance hall.

York, England

MIDDLETHORPE HALL

LUCINDA LAMBTON

Designed and built in the Queen Anne style in 1699, Middlethorpe Hall resembles the perfect doll house. Through the years, however, the property endured a checkered past, including a stint as a nightclub, leaving it in deplorable condition. Middlethorpe suffered many architectural indignities, including the insertion of steel beams and posts to support a dance floor, disco lighting and loud speakers. Historic House Hotels rescued Middlethorpe Hall in 1980, and has re-created the house which today sets the standard for old country house conversions.

Middlethorpe Hall's symmetrical design was constructed of mellow red brick with cream stone dressings and rustic quoins (cornerstones). The stone-flagged entry hall provides a warm greeting for guests who are then led to the staircase hall, dominated by a magnificent carved oak staircase with balusters. The drawing room, originally a ballroom for the former owners' family entertainment, is furnished with eighteenth-century elegance.

Of the thirty-one bedrooms, eleven are on two floors. These rooms have four-poster beds and suites with trompe l'oeil windows that show a view of local horse racing. Fifteen individually designed bedrooms and two suites are located in the Classical Courtyard, the original eighteenth-century stable block adjacent to the hotel.

The interior design is not grand and intimidating, but rather comfortable and welcoming—just what one would hope to find in an elegant private house.

Each of Middlethorpe's rooms reflects the elegance of the late seventeenth century when the house was built.

The dining room's handsome yellow and cornflower-blue furnishings.

The Laura Ashley ownership is evident throughout the manor's interiors.

Llangoed Hall's east façade faces pastoral surroundings.

Wye Valley, Mid Wales

LLANGOED HALL

Formerly known as Llangoed Castle, this comfortable and overstuffed country house hotel is set in 10 acres of garden and parkland. Redesigned by the celebrated Welsh architect Sir Clough Williams-Ellis in 1912, the style was called Edwardian house party. Although the property has been operating as a luxury hotel since 1990, it is thought to have been the site of various houses since as far back as 560 A.D. At one point, it is said that the first Welsh Parliament was held here and for several centuries it served as an Episcopal Grange. Rebuilt in 1632 in the classic Jacobean manor house style, parts of the south-facing wing, including the paneled library and the beautiful arched Jacobean porch, still remain. The present building was completed in 1919.

The structure was built of locally dressed stone and its original slate roof was so weighty, it had to be supported by steel girders. The interior architecture features a magnificent dining room, a baronial hall with a massive Gothic chimney piece and a finely carved timber staircase. In the early 1970s Llangoed was in danger of demolition, but was saved because of its historical and architectural importance.

Llangoed Hall was purchased in 1986 by Sir Bernard Ashley, chairman of Laura Ashley PLC, with the intention of converting it into a country house hotel. Because the house had been allowed to become derelict, part of the building fell down during reconstruction. Hence, some smaller rooms were added.

The Laura Ashley influence can be seen throughout the mansion among the many deep and cushy sofas, the quilted bedspreads and the flower-papered walls. Of the twenty-three charming and sumptuous bedrooms, eight maintain four-poster beds. Llangoed Hall has no reception desk. Rather, guests are met on the drive upon arrival. And there is no bar: a butler can be summoned to serve drinks on a silver tray.

The richly paneled oak Library is one of the only surviving parts of the original Jacobean mansion.

Bodysgallen traces its origins to a thirteenth-century watchtower.

Situated within 200 acres of private Welsh parkland, Bodysgallen Hall represents the best of Europe's lovingly restored country house hotels. Bodysgallen traces its origins to a thirteenth-century watchtower, now reached by a narrow winding stone staircase. The tower was built on the hillside to overlook Conwy Castle. In the seventeenth century, the main part of the magnificent stone manor house was built.

In 1980, Historic House Hotels acquired the decaying and sadly neglected mansion—investing two years towards its transformation into a splendid country

Llandudno, North Wales

BODYSGALLEN HALL

house hotel. The twentieth-century restoration and interior design have been carried out to emphasize the natural stately beauty of the house while the antiques, furniture and paintings have been chosen to create warm and comfortable surroundings. A maze of corridors and stairs winds through the building's interior. The hotel has nineteen bedrooms in the main house and nine cottage suites on the grounds—many with their own private gardens. Two of the finest rooms in the house are

the large oak-paneled entrance hall and the drawing room on the first floor, which displays splendid fireplaces and magnificent windows with stone mullions. The appropriate down-cushioned and chintz-covered sofas offer a cozy place for warm scones and tea on a rainy afternoon.

Each of the unique guest quarters are designed for comfort and elegance and all have their own private Edwardian bathroom. Nine cottages, with picturesque names such as Pineapple Lodge, Dove Cottage and the Gingerbread House are grouped around a secluded garden courtyard.

In addition to the hotel's architecture and design, magnificent views of the fabled peaks of Snowdownia and fabulous formal gardens, which include a Dutch Knot garden and a lily pond, spread through its windows.

The rare seventeenth-century Dutch Knot garden displays box hedges filled with sweet-scented herbs.

The twentieth-century restoration and interior design have been carried out to emphasize the natural stately beauty of the house while the antiques, furniture and paintings were chosen to create warm and comfortable surroundings.

Down-cushioned and chintz-covered sofas offer a cozy place to enjoy warm scones and tea on a rainy afternoon.

CASTLE HOTELS

CHAPTER IV

The 900-year-old stone walls of Amberley Castle were designed to protect the original occupants.

West Sussex, England

AMBERLEY CASTLE

Amberley Castle is just as King Arthur would have imagined it—900-year-old walls of stone 60 feet tall; a turreted lookout tower flying the castle flag; and a dungeon guarded by a heavy iron grille.

Somewhere around the year 1100, the Bishop of Chichester built the manor house at Amberley. However, it wasn't until the fourteenth century that the great surrounding wall was built to protect the resident bishop from marauding peasants and even pirates who could sail up the River Arun from the sea. Home improvements have been made to the castle throughout the centuries, but one of the most dramatic was made in the early 1500s when the dining hall was divided into two floors, thus creating the splendid Queen's Room with its barrel-vaulted ceiling and graceful lancet windows. In 1686, after a visit to Amberley Castle by King Charles II, a hunting mural depicting the King and his Queen Catherine was added to the walls of the Queen's Room.

In order to prevent some of the fourteen massive guest rooms from appearing too austere or overwhelming, the owners draped Laura Ashley fabrics and plush carpets over the centuries-old château stone providing

One of the guest suites features centuries-old lancet windows and comfortable furnishings.

character, charm and warmth. Each bedroom is named after a Sussex castle and all have been individually designed to reflect the character of that room—some featuring beautiful antique canopied beds and lace curtains. Several rooms have private access to the battlements.

Until 1989, this magical building had always been a private residence—concealing its lovely gardens and stately rooms from the public. Now, even commoners with credit cards can experience the castle interiors which were designed by the owners to be both luxurious and opulent, yet homey and welcoming.

Stone floors and genuine suits of armor adorn the entry hall.

Several of the bedrooms feature antique canopied beds covered in Laura Ashley fabrics.

Hotel Schloss Mönchstein is considered by many to be the world's finest urban sanctuary.

The fifteenth-century chapel is the perfect setting for a romantic wedding.

Salzburg, Austria

HOTEL SCHLOSS MÖNCHSTEIN

Touted by many as the finest urban sanctuary of the world, this fourteenth-century, Gothic castle features just seven rooms and ten apartments. Each room is decorated with fine period antiques and provided with all the comforts available to create a uniquely elegant atmosphere.

Built in 1358 on top of a hill overlooking the heart of downtown Salzburg, Mönchstein Castle was originally designed to host guests of the archbishops. In the mid-1600s it became an estate of the University of Salzburg, serving as a professorial retreat. It wasn't until 1948 that it was transformed into the hotel it has been run as ever since.

One of the best features of this five-star deluxe hotel is that every room is unique in decor, furnishings and layout, and every guest room has a private bath. The interiors were designed by owners Baron and Baroness von Mierka who have owned the property since 1956. A favorite bedroom is the turreted Tower Suite which provides a Rapunzelesque view of Salzburg.

The salon features comfortable overstuffed seating, and antique furnishings with historic paintings and fine Oriental carpets. The hotel's restaurant is famous for both its decor and cuisine. The dining room features exquisite leaded windows, dark wood paneling and red tapestry walls. A large painting of Emperor Franz Joseph watches majestically over the room. The castle also features a fifteenth-century chapel, perfect for intimate weddings in a very romantic setting.

The ivy-covered castle is surrounded by a lush private park creating its secluded setting. The center of the old city can be reached within ten minutes by using a mountainside elevator.

The hotel's dining room features magnificent leaded glass windows and excellent cuisine.

Each room is decorated with fine period antiques and provided with all the comforts available to create a uniquely elegant atmosphere.

Neckarwestheim, Germany

SCHLOSSHOTEL LIEBENSTEIN

If you've dreamed of staying in a true fairy-tale castle, Schlosshotel Liebenstein can provide the experience. Set on a hillside with a view of the neighboring vineyards, this castle hotel offers twenty-four luxurious rooms and suites, with modern recreation and conference facilities.

The well-preserved, predominantly renaissance castle also shows Gothic and Roman origins. From the dome vaults to the typically German painted ceilings and window surrounds, this gem exudes the handcrafted artisan commitment. Upon entering each room, one notices the style and craftsmanship of the medieval carpenter.

Even though it features a twelfth-century watchtower, the castle was built in the middle of the thirteenth century. It was originally owned by the Swabian Knightly Order of Liebenstein. The largest part of the main castle was not built until the first quarter of the seventeenth century. The property features a rare one-hundred-person chapel built in 1599 which today serves as a stylish surrounding for cultural occasions and splendid weddings.

Sport, leisure and recreation abound at Liebenstein. The 27-hole golf course on the castle grounds is considered to be one of the finest in Germany.

A comfortable bedroom features Gothic style furnishings and exquisite European feather beds.

If you've dreamed of staying in a true fairy-tale castle, Schlosshotel Liebenstein can provide the experience.

The castle's dining hall serves medieval meals fit for a king.

Many rooms feature well-preserved architectural details from the past, including vaulted ceilings and stone archways.

Each of the hotel's eighty-four rooms feature unique furnishings varying from antique period pieces to contemporary European styling.

Salzburg, Austria

HOTEL SCHLOSS FUSCHL

Hotel Schloss Fuschl has been called a haven of relaxation and a hub of elegance located in Austria's most beautiful landscape. Jutting idyllically onto Lake Fuschl, with panoramic views of the Salzkammergut mountains, this fifteenth-century castle is today divided into a hotel, spa and beauty retreat compound.

Built in 1450 by the archbishops of Salzburg, this enchanting castle has maintained its worthy reputation as a romantic mountain refuge. Originally constructed as an exclusive retreat and hunting lodge, it was once the venue of magnificent hunts and feasts. Through the years it occasionally lost position and suffered from decaying walls and cobwebs. Ownership changed as it was sold and rented, confiscated and auctioned. The end to such unsteady circumstances came in 1948 when Schloss Fuschl was transformed into a hotel and restaurant. It was again acquired in 1977 by a hotel group that converted it into a luxury hotel with all modern amenities. Today, the "tower above the lake" flourishes with outdoor tennis courts, a 9-hole golf course, fishing, sailing and skiing.

The castle cellars have been carefully restored to include a marble swimming pool under vaulted ceilings.

Secular and ecclesiastical princes once retreated to this castle to relax, and even today the rooms of the main building offer a truly royal atmosphere. Many rooms feature well-preserved architectural details from the past. The main castle's vaulted ceilings, stone archways and columns co-exist with centuries-old stone floors. Elaborate antique wrought iron details abound. Even the castle cellars have been carefully restored to include a marble swimming pool.

Each of the hotel's eighty-four rooms feature unique furnishings varying from antique period pieces to contemporary European styling. Guests have several lodging opportunities, from the romantic castle and comfortable bungalows on the shore to the old hunting lodge and rustic Jagdhof furnished in the original style of the region.

Built as a hunting lodge in 1450, this enchanting castle has maintained its reputation as a romantic mountain refuge.

The living areas feature vaulted ceilings, antique terra-cotta floors, and furnishings that date to the sixteenth century.

Monte Vibiano's surrounding parkland includes tennis courts, lush ancient vegetation and a beautiful swimming pool.

Mercatello, Italy

VILLA DI MONTE VIBIANO

In the heart of Umbria, amid cultivations of tobacco and olives, sits a hilltop hamlet and the Villa di Monte Vibiano. After many centuries, this imposing castle has become an eclectic combination of styles: a stone façade with two towers, Romanesque capitals under the portico and renaissance loggias.

Monte Vibiano's origins date back to the first century B.C. when a family of Roman patricians established themselves on this enchanting site. It has since seen many architectural forms and changes.

The present form of the building was constructed around 1500. In 1920, an Umbrian nobleman—and grandfather of the present owner—began a ten-year restoration which maintained the original integrity of the castle while adapting it to modern needs. The medieval arches and colonnades, vaulted ceilings, enormous limestone fireplaces, a frescoed dining room and ancient terra-cotta floors still remain. Among other interesting features of Villa di Monte Vibiano are the ancient wine cellars and an antique collection of rare ceramic tiles. The interiors are tastefully furnished with antiques dating from 1500, including a magnificent tapestry based on a Rubens design.

The property now serves as both a residence and hotel with six carefully appointed bedrooms. The surrounding parkland includes a swimming pool, tennis court and lush, ancient vegetation. There is also a small labyrinth and a summer theater.

The peaceful and luxurious environment is what most of all gives Monte Vibiano the charm of a private residence. The hotel is open only from June through September.

The Villa di Monte Vibiano
is comfortably decorated
with antiques.

The enormous limestone fireplace remains from the original form of the building, constructed around 1500.

The peaceful and luxurious environment is what most of all gives the Villa di Monte Vibiano the charm of a private residence.

The interior design utilizes a warm and quiet decor of green and natural whites.

Baarn, The Netherlands

KASTEEL DE HOOGE VUURSCHE

The Kasteel's magnificent gardens, ponds and fountains took a lot of care and time to complete.

Noted for its beautifully sculpted gables and architectural details, the Kasteel de Hooge Vuursche, finished in 1911, required an extensive building period for its time; all of the artwork and exquisite interior architectural details were created on-site. Commissioned by an ex-merchant navy officer, the building still shows the influence of the sea and seamanship in some of its interior design.

Located near Amsterdam, the castle served as a backdrop for many glittering parties in its early years. It remained in the same family until 1975 when it was purchased by Heineken Breweries.

In 1986, the Dutch castle was converted into a luxury hotel, a fitting reminder of its elegant past. The property has been well preserved in the traditional manner as the twenty-four rooms attest—each a work of art with detailed plaster works and intricate murals. The elegance of this estate is evident in its many loving details including the hand-carved woodwork, leaded glass windows and parquet floors. The interior design utilizes a warm and quiet decor of green and natural whites.

The Kasteel de Hooge Vuursche sits amid 36 acres of magnificent gardens, ponds and fountains which took a great amount of care and time to perfect. The gardens were designed by the then famous landscape architect Tersteeg from Naarden. There is a pond on the east side, surrounded by elegant masonry and beautiful shrubs and trees.

Each of the Kasteel's rooms
are a work of art, evident in
many loving details.

MANOR HOUSES
CHAPTER V

The ivy-covered façade provides an inviting entry.

The Oval Room is one of thirty-two unique bedrooms.

The elegant indoor pool of Bishopstrow House.

The Morning Room was originally the library of the manor.

Wiltshire, England

BISHOPSTROW HOUSE

Bishopstrow House is a special gem in the crown of English country house hotels. The elegant Georgian manor house was designed by John Pinch of nearby Bath and built in 1817. In 1978 the house was renovated and sympathetically converted into a hotel.

Set amid 27 acres of Wiltshire countryside, Bishopstrow House is surrounded by magnificent English gardens which feature a Doric temple built of chilmark stone in 1770. The ivy-covered façade softens this historically rated manor house which now consists of thirty-two richly appointed bedrooms. The elegant hotel features impressive public rooms containing English and French antiques, nineteenth-century oil paintings and Persian carpets. Each of the public spaces are decorated with rich colors and yards of chintz.

Listed Grade-I for its historic and architectural importance, Hartwell House is an eclectic building with both Jacobean and Georgian façades. The interiors contain outstanding decorative plaster work, ceilings, and paneling. The quality of its architecture is complemented by the paintings and antique furniture which now decorate its elegant and spacious rooms.

Hartwell House is a hotel with a past. It was built in the sixteenth century by the Lee family, ancestors of General Robert E. Lee. Its most famous resident was Louis XVIII, exiled King of France, who leased the house in 1809 for five years. The king signed his accession papers to the throne of France in the library. In 1938 the estate was purchased from the Lee family for preservation by the philanthropist Ernest E. Cook (grandson of the famous travel agent Thomas Cook) who made Hartwell House and its park available to Historic House Hotels for complete restoration and conversion.

Upon entering Hartwell House, visitors first encounter the Great Hall, an imposing room in English baroque style built in 1740. To the left of the Great Hall is an oak paneled room, now the bar, hung with paintings of the early eighteenth-century gardens. The rococo Morning Room, with its magnificently decorated ceiling and door casings, and the adjacent drawing room and library are all Georgian, built around 1760. A dramatic Gothic hall and staircase with Jacobean carved figures lead to thirty-two bedrooms and suites on three floors. The stable block has additional rooms. Hartwell House also has a magnificent health spa with swimming pool and beauty salon.

The façade of Hartwell House is designed in both Jacobean and Georgian styles.

Buckinghamshire, England

HARTWELL HOUSE

The Great Hall's floor is laid with Portland stone. The room contains magnificent examples of plaster work.

The Morning Room features outstanding rococo plaster work. This ceiling narrowly escaped destruction in the fire of 1973.

The distinguished and comfortable library contains some of the finest surviving gilt-brass wiring in Britain.

The creeper-clad gray stone mansion with its turrets, tall chimneys and arched windows of leaded glass.

Kent, England

EASTWELL MANOR

The manor retains an air of its one-thousand-year history with stone carved fireplaces, leather chesterfields and fine antique pieces.

Eastwell Manor, a mock-Jacobean mansion with a gray stone façade, storybook turrets, tall chimneys and arched windows of leaded glass can be glimpsed at each turn of a long tree-lined drive. This manor-turned-hotel stands on 3,000 acres of farm and parkland where local sheep can be seen grazing peacefully. From the terrace at the rear of the manor, a series of stone steps with curved balustrades leads down through the formal Italian gardens to a magnificent fountain with stone dolphins. On the side, immaculately clipped hedges and fragrant roses proliferate.

The first historical mention of this Norman manor house was in the *Domesday Book* for the year 1069. Eastwell Manor has had a colorful history including several royal connections such as the distinction of having two queens to the manor born—Queen Beatrice of Spain and Queen Marie of Romania.

The manor changed hands several times throughout history. It was in 1928 that a new owner completely rebuilt it to its present form. During the Second World War the house was taken over by the Seventh Armoured Division and tanks replaced sheep on the pastureland. Winston Churchill used the lake to test an amphibious tank.

Although completely renovated in 1980, the manor still retains an air of 1920s opulence; huge fireplaces with carved stone mantle arches characterize the interiors of Eastwell. From the flagstone covered great hall, a carved staircase leads up to twenty-three bedrooms with bath—all of immense proportion. The rooms are luxuriously furnished in traditional style. Each of the rooms have been named for previous owners or famous people associated with the manor throughout the ages.

All of Eastwell Manor's rooms are luxuriously furnished in traditional style.

The Bayeaux Suite is a secluded, richly paneled room with a tranquil atmosphere.

Located just 30 minutes from Hyde Park Corner, Gravetye Manor is recognized as one of the top three country house hotels in England, a land dotted with such establishments. Located atop a splendid hill surrounded by 1,000 acres of land, the manor overlooks a steep-sided valley leading to a private trout lake. This Elizabethan stone manor features twin gables and such Victorian details as stone-mullioned windows with deep reveals, copings, finials, a stone roof and deep window seats.

Gravetye Manor has had many owners who have each played a part in making it the charming place it is today. The manor was built in 1598 by Richard Infield for his bride Katharine. Today, the initials "R" and "K" can still be seen in the stone over the main entrance door. Also, their portraits are carved in oak over the fireplace in the master bedroom.

William Robinson, one of the great gardeners of all time, bought the manor and the thousand acres on which it stands in 1884. It became his personal residence until his death in 1935. At Gravetye he realized many of his ideas for the creation of the English natural garden of which he was the pioneer. The variety and charm of the arrangement of trees and shrubs and the

West Sussex, England

GRAVETYE MANOR

The variety and charm of the arrangement of trees and shrubs, and the landscaping and layout of the different garden types at Gravetye Manor are a memorial to William Robinson.

The "Hansel and Gretel" manor is filled with a hint of smoking wood fires and the scent of floral blooms from the vases of fresh flowers.

landscaping and layout of the different garden types at Gravetye are, to this day, his memorial. Robinson also restored the old house to its original beauty and dignity, adding oak paneling from the estate forests. Today each of the guest rooms are named for trees on the estate instead of being numbered.

Robinson's simple good taste was unusual for one who might be described as late Victorian. He wrote several books about the property, which are kept in the manor today, detailing his fascination with many aspects of the house.

Captivated by Robinson's house and setting, hotelier Peter Herbert arrived in 1957 and set about creating a luxury country house hotel. It is his commitment that makes guests feel as if they really are staying in someone else's house. The "Hansel and Gretel" manor is filled with a hint of smoking wood fires and the scent of floral blooms from the vases of fresh flowers. The now eighteen-room hotel and its interiors were lovingly furnished through the direction of designer Juliet Percy of Pierott Designs in Sussex. Each room has its own design and character with fabrics chosen to suit the room. All the furnishings are original Edwardian to Elizabethan antiques, and fine paintings abound.

The oak-carved portraits of the original owners of Gravetye Manor can still be seen over the fireplace in the Master Bedroom.

The restaurant at Gravetye Manor is decorated with original antiques.

The "Walnut" Bedroom is in the North Wing. Each of Gravetye's rooms has its own design and character, and each guest room is named for trees on the estate instead of being numbered.

The Crabtree & Evelyn room
features wonderful botanical
prints and a
floral bedspread.

Stapleford Park Country House Hotel is one of the most important stately homes to be converted into a hotel. Historically the seat of the Earls of Harborough, this 450-year-old home was once used as a Victorian hunting lodge. If a unique and historic country house experience is on your list, certainly Stapleford Park is the place to visit.

The Stapleford has only been operating as a hotel since 1988 when Americans Bob and Wendy Payton fell in love with an idyllic style of country life and this country mansion of eclectic architectural style. Architect Bob Weighton, who specializes in country house conversions, was given the task of converting this Grade-I listed building into a luxury hotel. In addition to totally new plumbing and wiring, Weighton created new bedrooms, new kitchens and a replacement roof for the sixteenth-century section. This stately home was built essentially Edwardian and Georgian, but was never quite completed. Throughout the years, however, additions were built including a seventeenth-century wing possessing a curious mix of the latest in Stuart classicism and romantic medievalism. After three years of renovation, some declared the new style an unconventional approach to traditional hotel design.

The Paytons knew that interior designer Anne Charlton of Sloane Decorators would know exactly which fabrics and wall coverings were needed for the public spaces—which Bob Payton hoped would possess the air of a Victorian gentleman's hunting lodge. But Payton also had a unique idea for decorating the guest rooms. He had each of the thirty-five bedrooms individually designed by renowned arbiters of style who were given the direction of providing sumptuous comfort. These Signature Bedrooms were uniquely created

Buckinghamshire, England

STAPLEFORD PARK COUNTRY HOUSE HOTEL

Historically the seat of
the Earls of Harborough,
this 450-year-old home
was once used as a
Victorian hunting lodge.

Each of the thirty-five bedrooms were individually designed by renowned arbiters of style.

by established designers such as Nina Campbell, Jane Churchill, David Hicks and Lindka Cierach (dress designer to the Duchess of York). Other room designers were from such noted shops as Crabtree & Evelyn, Tiffany's, Liberty, Turnbull & Asser, Max Pike and Wedgwood. The result of this experiment created a veritable interior designers' museum and a truly wonderful tourist attraction.

Conservation was one of the Paytons' interests when refurbishing the seventeenth-century home. Among the preserved treasures are the dining room's wonderful Grinling Gibbons (the famous seventeenth-century woodcarver) designs, the original rich mahogany paneling that graces the main hall and staircase, and an Oriental carpet that once belonged to former Stapleford owner, Lord Gretton. Old and new furnishings live happily together: pimento red and mint green leather chesterfield sofas are placed with rescued olive green ones. Other light touches include breakfast table settings of Wedgwood's Peter Rabbit nursery ware rather than a more formal porcelain. According to the Paytons, the goal was to create an informality a little different from traditional English hospitality.

The Lady Gretton Room was designed by Anne Charlton using specially fabricated black tartan from Scotland.

The Stapleford Park Country House Hotel sits on parkland designed by Capability Brown.

Culloden House Hotel sits on 40 acres of lush Scottish parkland.

It is believed that Culloden House was designed by Robert Adam, the great Scottish neoclassical architect.

Inverness, Scotland

CULLODEN HOUSE HOTEL

Visitors to Culloden House step back into history as they are welcomed into this private mansion. Princes past and present have enjoyed the ambiance and hospitality of this elegant Palladian mansion that rises out of the morning mist across an enormous expanse of lawn.

The house was owned by the Forbes family of Culloden who maintained ownership from 1626 to 1923. It is believed that the seventeenth-century mansion was designed by Robert Adam, the great Scottish neoclassical architect. The house was rebuilt in 1772 after the original Jacobean castle was largely destroyed by fire in 1753. Built of warm gray stone, the house features a large central block and two pavilions, protected by 40 acres of parkland.

The interiors feature high ceilings, ornate plaster decor including magnificent griffins, huge thick pelmeted curtains, and rooms with comfy furniture which softens the grandeur. Everywhere silver and highly polished wood gleam amid the flower arrangements. The twenty-three bedrooms, most recently refurbished, are well appointed. Some have four-poster beds. Opulent bathrooms have gold-plated fittings, huge baths and spacious showers.

A blending of classic French and Scottish country house cuisine is served in the luxurious dining rooms.

As the sun sets on the summer lawn of Culloden House, the plaintive notes of a Scottish piper in full Highland regalia fill the air before dinner. As one would expect, the hotel's cuisine is outstanding—a blending of classic French and Scottish country house fare. Service, too, fits into the par excellence category from hoteliers Ian and Marjory McKenzie. It is their extra personal touch that has brought guests from around the world since 1981.

Glistening chandeliers, marble fireplaces, massive pillars and classic plaster reliefs feature in the decor of the house.

Each bedroom in Culloden House is uniquely decorated.

Opulent bathrooms have gold-plated fittings, huge baths and spacious showers.

GREAT ESCAPES

CHAPTER VI

The Hotel Pitrizza looks as if it were carved into the rocky beach of the Costa Smeralda.

Sardinia, Italy

HOTEL PITRIZZA

O ften described as one of the world's unique hotels, the Hotel Pitrizza looks as if it were carved into the rocky beach of the Costa Smeralda.

Built in 1964, the hotel was designed by Milanese architect Luigi Vietti who is responsible for most of the rustic buildings on the Costa Smeralda and in particular, the village of Porvo Cervo. The design can only be described as understated, but elegant simplicity. From its rough plaster walls to the granite details, this hotel looks indigenous to the area. The Pitrizza actually has more the air of a private club than a hotel. It is the ideal place for a quiet and relaxing holiday.

The property consists of twelve villas each of which has between four and six bedrooms and private terraces. Each villa is unique, but all feature thick white plaster walls and magnificent exposed juniper beams. The interiors were supervised by Susanne Magliano who made effective use of local Sardinian handicrafts such as carved wooden antique chests, woven woolen carpets, curtains, tapestries, cushion covers and bedspreads—all incorporating the local designs of animals and flowers.

The Clubhouse, located in the center of the resort, features the reception area and restaurant, and access to the beach and dramatic seawater swimming pool, carved out of the rocks. The views from the terrace overlook the sea and beyond to Corsica where even in June the snow-topped mountain peaks are frequently visible.

Each of the Pitrizza's villas are unique, but all feature magnificent exposed juniper beams and thick white plaster walls.

From its rough plaster walls to the granite details, the hotel looks indigenous to the area.

The views from the terrace overlook the sea and beyond to Corsica where even in June, the snow-topped mountain peaks are frequently visible.

L'Impérial Palace's fabulous location prompted the town of Annecy and others to invest in its complete renovation.

Snowy white window treatments billow like sails in the hotel's elegant La Voile restaurant.

A meeting room in L'Impérial Palace features state-of-the-art equipment in a comfortable atmosphere.

Annecy, France

L'IMPÉRIAL PALACE

In 1990, the completely renovated L'Impérial Palace, located just 40 kilometers from the Geneva airport, opened its doors once again. Only the façade of this eighty-year-old hotel remains the same; the interiors are completely different. What was once a sumptuous grande dame, filled with gold embroidered velvet curtains and heavy moldings is now contemporary, with art deco undertones. The interiors were gutted, giving way for the installation of modern and necessary conveniences such as air conditioning, computer terminals, simultaneous translation systems, audio-visual systems and television security. Even an escalator was installed for the waiters, linking the main kitchen and the restaurants—a first for French hotels.

To make room for a casino and conference center and to make guests more comfortable, the room count was cut from three hundred in the original layout to just ninety-nine guest rooms. The hotel commands spectacular views, as it is located at the tip of a peninsula on Lake Annecy—the clearest lake in Europe. Nearly all rooms overlook Lake Annecy and the Savoy Alps, as well as the surrounding lush green parkland with its hundred-year-old trees.

When L'Impérial Palace opened in the summer of 1913, it attracted an elegant and royal clientele who came to experience the lake and its surroundings. During World War II, it was occupied by both the Italian and German armies who used it as a hospital. It reopened after the war and functioned again in its original splendor. During the 1960s, tastes changed and demand for this style of hotel declined. In 1965 L'Impérial Palace closed its doors. But, because of its unique site, the town of Annecy bought the land and building and set about to find investors to remodel the hotel. The renovation was given all the taste and care that the hotel deserved.

The guest rooms and suites
are contemporary, well lit,
well appointed and
designed for comfort.

The hotel's belle epoque façade was built in 1908.

Saint Jean Cap-Ferrat, France

GRAND HÔTEL DU CAP-FERRAT

From its beginning in 1908, the Grand Hôtel du Cap-Ferrat has attracted the international elite who winter on the Riviera. Princes and dukes of the Russian Imperial family and the other European royal houses, lords and barons from England, the great entrepreneurs of finance and industry, celebrities and literary and artistic figures, as well as the merely rich and famous have sojourned to this famous hotel for decades. Although the hotel has been renovated and updated, what remains unchanged is its essence of style, superb service and immaculate environment.

Located on 14 acres of azure Mediterranean beach property, this hotel was built in belle epoque style, and was destined to become legendary as one of the greatest rendezvous spots in the world. It is ideally located amid private villas and adjacent to Nice and Monte Carlo.

Recently, a major renovation was completed by the London-based design firm Wilson Gregory Aeberhard who specialize in hotel interior design. The entire fifty-nine-room hotel and public spaces were renovated to include a sophisticated decor using the finest materials available, including murals, silks, frescoes, mosaics and artwork throughout. The new color palette combines pastel tones with subtle shades of Provençe and white-washed pine furniture. The new look of the public areas was inspired by the local landscape and the four seasons, as the hotel is now open all year-round. The elegant glass ceiling of the rotunda was restored to its former glory and the grand villa concept renewed.

The Le Cap restaurant is
renowned by major
gastronomical guides.
The chef raises the culinary
art to great heights, using
ingredients and influences
from the region.

The guest rooms were
decorated with traditional
furnishings around the subtle
shades of Provençe.

Located on 14 acres of
azure Mediterranean
beach property, the
Grand Hôtel du Cap-Ferrat
was destined to become
legendary as one of the
greatest rendevous spots
in the world.

The southern exposure was designed to bring sunshine into this mountain hotel.

Spacious bedrooms feature warm oak wood, floral wallpaper and hand-carved and painted armoires.

Gstaad, Switzerland

GRAND HOTEL PARK

One of the newer luxury hotels in Switzerland is really an old hotel at heart. Reopened in 1990, the five-star Grand Hotel Park in the resort village of Gstaad occupies the grounds of the former Park Hotel of the early 1900s. The new hotel, built by a Swiss industrialist, is dedicated to the best in quality and tradition, both in the hotel's ambiance and in its impeccable service.

The details of the complete redesign were carried out by architects S. Jaggi of Gstaad and W. Schaepper of Boston. They designed the exterior to face south for maximum sunshine and light. The hotel features natural stone and wood construction throughout. The architecture is typical Swiss chalet style with terraces. The interiors and furnishings were specifically designed for the hotel and reflect the local Bernese style. The hotel has ninety-three luxuriously large bedrooms that feature awe-inspiring views of the Gstaad landscape. Each bathroom is covered in pink Portuguese marble and includes separate shower and bath.

The design of the public spaces and the Grand Restaurant was dictated by the warmth of the mountain style. The public spaces feature light oak wood-paneled walls and elegantly comfortable furnishings; the Grand Restaurant focuses on rich wood-paneled walls, wood ceilings and a parquet floor. Elegant fabrics and traditional style make for a sophisticated yet relaxed atmosphere. The focal point of the lobby area is an antique wrought-iron lift, taken from the former Park Hotel Reuteler, which features a combination of art deco and Swiss style. The lobby is adorned by a Grommaire tapestry.

It is this combination of discreet luxury and traditional comfort blending with the surroundings that makes this a hotel destined to be among the best in Switzerland.

The Grand Restaurant is
elegantly appointed with
rich oak wood-paneled
walls, parquet floors and
moire taffeta drapes.

The Splendido's private balconies overlook the Italian Riviera's green hillside.

The Italian Riviera is not lacking for style or for hotels, but the Hotel Splendido in Portofino still maintains its distinguished reputation as a triumph of underplayed luxury in one of the most exclusive hotels in Italy. The accommodations are luxurious and the service superb; nevertheless there is a distinct atmosphere of informality.

The Splendido is not a Grand Hotel in the conventional sense—it is not filled with sumptuous fantasy and doesn't pretend to be a setting for elaborate social rituals. Instead, it strives to be quietly democratic. The public spaces are richly furnished with gilt consoles and Persian rugs, however, the room furnishings are comfortable. An ongoing renovation beginning in 1985 has allowed the interiors to compete with the magnificent views. Through French designer Gerard Gallet, the comfortable elegance of this four-story patrician villa is as dramatic on the inside as it is outside.

Portofino, Italy

HOTEL SPLENDIDO

This ancient sixteenth-century monastery-turned-hotel was built on an east-west axis following the contour of the hill. The Benedictine monks wanted their original monastery to attract the sun, however, it soon came to be a magnet for sea pirates and was eventually abandoned. Today the ocher and white exterior of the Splendido displays the sunny balconies of the sixty-three bedrooms, with their green-painted belle epoque wrought-iron furniture.

At the Splendido, the accomodations are luxurious and the service superb; nevertheless, there is a distinct atmosphere of informality.

After an extensive
renovation, the comfortable
interiors compete
with the views.

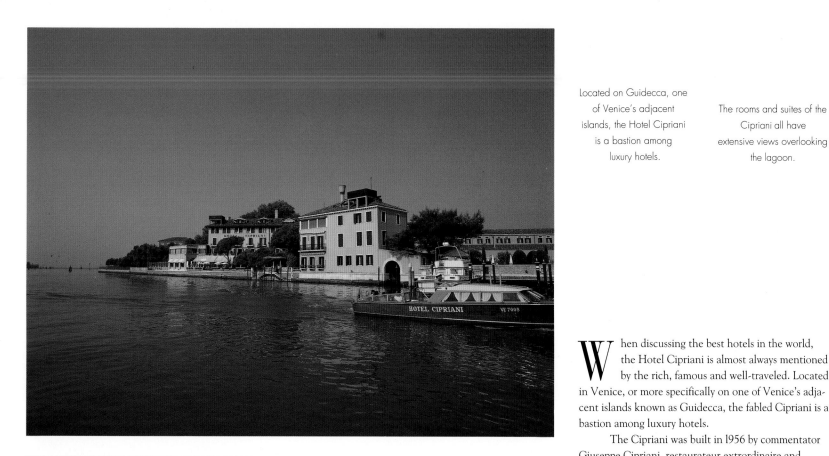

Located on Guidecca, one of Venice's adjacent islands, the Hotel Cipriani is a bastion among luxury hotels.

The rooms and suites of the Cipriani all have extensive views overlooking the lagoon.

A seating area is both elegant as expected and comfortable as a country house.

Venice, Italy

HOTEL CIPRIANI

When discussing the best hotels in the world, the Hotel Cipriani is almost always mentioned by the rich, famous and well-traveled. Located in Venice, or more specifically on one of Venice's adjacent islands known as Guidecca, the fabled Cipriani is a bastion among luxury hotels.

The Cipriani was built in 1956 by commentator Giuseppe Cipriani, restaurateur extrordinaire and better known as the founder of the famous Harry's Bar. Cipriani's dream had always been to build a luxurious hotel within easy reach of Venice's famous St. Mark's Square and yet far enough away to guarantee peace and privacy. After securing the Guinness family as financial partners, Cipriani built the hotel and acted as the management head. Covering a little more than 3 acres of rare and lush Venetian gardens (which were once a modest vineyard) the hotel was built in a low-slung resort architectural style and includes the only swimming pool in the city. The buildings are covered with beige-pink stucco and have terra-cotta tiled roofs, French doors and dark green shutters.

The hotel's decor is stylish throughout, with the suites and bedrooms ranging from simple elegance to grand opulence. All rooms have extensive views overlooking the lagoon. Some of the suites feature great indulgences, with several rooms, excesses of silk, extravagant bathrooms and wooden furniture with swirled pastel baroque twists tipped with gold. One of the most expensive suites in the hotel, the Nani, has baroque gilt furniture and antique parquetry.

The suites feature exquisite Venetian furnishings including silk fabrics and miles of marble.

The public spaces of the hotel are elegant, as expected, paved with marble and terrazzo and draped with Oriental rugs. But the feel is more like a country house hall—a big basket of freshly polished apples offers a greeting. There are wide staircases, miles of mahogany and exquisite art everywhere. Part of the hotel was redesigned by Parisian architect Gerard Gallet, whose other claim was the redesign of the Orient Express carriages. There are clever designs in the corridors—some barrel-vaulted, some russets and peaches—all cleverly lit. Most walls are fabric covered, often with Fortuny fabrics.

The Cipriani, however, is known as much for its service as for its style. Thanks to careful direction by Dr. Natale Rusconi, one of Europe's most famous hoteliers, guests will never hear the ringing of front desk bells or be asked to sign for anything consumed on premises. The staff makes it their business to know the guests. While at the Cipriani, your face is your signature.

Simple elegance distinguishes the guest rooms at the Cipriani.

The historic Hall of Knights provides an elegant setting for the most important business meetings.

In the entrance hall above the main staircase is an original stained glass window scene featuring St. Hubert, the patron saint of hunters.

Preserved in its original style, the Hunting Lodge de Mookerheide maintains much of its original art nouveau architecture and interior design.

Molenhoek, The Netherlands

HUNTING LODGE DE MOOKERHEIDE

At the turn of the twentieth century, a local baron bought 333 acres of land between the German border and an area of Holland known as Maas Valley. It was here, in 1903, that he built his excellent hunting lodge and personal estate complete with stables, kennels for a pack of hounds, and a pheasant, guinea fowl and partridge farm to provide game for the shoot. Known to the locals as the Jugendstill castle, this property sits high atop a hillside at Mookerheide. Through the years this elegant art nouveau style property changed hands and at one time even became the property of an order of Catholic nuns. It wasn't until 1987 that the Hunting Lodge de Mookerheide became an intimate luxury hotel.

Preserved in its original style, the property today still features much of its original art nouveau architecture and interior design. In the entrance hall above the main staircase is an original stained glass window scene depicting St. Hubert, the patron saint of hunters. Several other magnificent stained glass windows appear throughout the castle. Each of the seven rooms feature unique decor. Some look as if they're part of a fairy tale. The tower restaurant has been noted as a first class establishment, and on a clear day one can see several villages through its windows. In the historic tradition of the building, the kitchen excels at preparing a wide range of venison and game dishes.

Game is still a favorite feature of the lodge. Among the 24 acres of magnificent parkland surrounding the hotel exists a deer park and herb and vegetable garden. Leisure activities can include an extensive survey of the surrounding forests and moors or a visit to the nearby golf course.

The à la carte
restaurant
serves fine cuisine
prepared with home
grown vegetables
and herbs from
Mookerheide's
own garden.

The wine cellar of the
Hunting Lodge de
Mookerheide.

Stained glass windows
grace bathrooms with
beauty and luxury.

HISTORIC CHÂTEAUX

CHAPTER VII

The château was
constructed in 1760 of
white limestone and pink
brick, typical of the region's
rococo architecture of
that time.

Remaisnil's interiors are
furnished with eighteenth-
century antiques and
tapestries.

Doullens, France

CHÂTEAU DE REMAISNIL

At Château de Remaisnil, one can experience the elegance of château life in the ambiance of a private eighteenth-century château. Excellent French cuisine can be enjoyed, along with the enormous richness of French culture, art and architecture, in one of the most historic regions in France.

The château was constructed in 1760 of white limestone and pink brick, typical of the region's rococo architecture of the time. The interiors are furnished with eighteenth-century antiques and tapestries. Chandeliers and sconces are lit with candles, not electricity. Throughout history the Château de Remaisnil has passed through several families. It was lovingly restored in 1980 by proprietors Bernard and Laura Ashley. By 1987, the château had new owners who began lending it for small meetings and to individual guests.

Each of the château's twenty bedrooms are lavishly decorated, and all have bathrooms. The rest of the château—the coach house, library, salons, dining, billiard and conference rooms—is exquisitely decorated with antique furnishings.

The Château de Remaisnil is a rare blend of the warmth and ambiance of a private home and the facilities of a luxury hotel.

Original architecture has
been complemented by
interiors done by Laura
Ashley, with the intent
of keeping the
historical context.

The library provides a
comfortable setting for
guests.

Bedrooms are romantically
designed to ensure the
ambiance of an
elegant country home.

The pool room with vaulted ceilings, travertine floors and Palladian windows overlooks the Tyrrhenian Sea.

Built as a guest house for Castle Odescalchi, La Posta Vecchia was designed by Vanvitelli in 1640.

Palo Laziale, Italy

LA POSTA VECCHIA

The difference between an Italian country villa and a renaissance palace is perspective. But if an awe-inspiring palace environment alongside the tranquil Mediterranean sounds inviting, La Posta Vecchia is the place to visit.

Built as a guest house for Castle Odescalchi, La Posta Vecchia was designed by Vanvitelli in 1640. The renaissance palace sits atop the ruins of two second-century imperial Roman villas—the remains of which can still be seen in a private archaeological museum. The Umber Villa was once used as a posting house for the exchange of horses, hence the property name. Today La Posta Vecchia is a five-star luxury hotel on 8 lush acres of garden 20 miles from Rome.

The atmosphere of La Posta Vecchia is unlike the typical hostelry. Until recently, it was the Italian residence of billionaire J. Paul Getty. Filled with priceless seventeenth-century furnishings personally chosen by Getty, the residence could be considered a museum if it weren't for the rich comfortable sofas, Fortuny curtains and plush Persian rugs. Art abounds in the eighteen lavishly appointed bedrooms. The Medici Suite features a bed which was formerly an altar, and the dowry chest of Maria de Medici. Upon arrival, guests are greeted by the stone-flagged entrance hall flanked by marble busts of Roman emperors and two magnificent tapestries designed by Raphael.

Gilt, velvet and rare antique marble flourish in La Posta Vecchia. The ceilings are magnificently coffered and almost every room (including bathrooms) has a fireplace. Renaissance details, including stone door lintels and sculptures still exist. The dining room, cloaked with Fortuny drapes that brush polished terracotta floors, features an elegant 20-foot Sienese marble table set with Genori china. Everywhere exists the old-world elegance that one would expect of this renaissance Roman palace.

Centuries of treasures adorn
the Salon with its coffered
ceiling and polished
terra-cotta floors.

The Medici Suite features a
pink marble bath and gilt
mirror positioned so the
bather is visible from the
adjoining bedroom.

The romantic Medici Suite's
blue velvet bed was once
an altar piece.

With light shining from
crystal chandeliers, the
dining room serves the finest
in traditional French cuisine
in an elegant atmosphere.

The exterior of the
Château de Bellinglise
shows its origins as a
sixteenth-century castle.

Elincourt-Sainte-Marguerite, France

CHÂTEAU DE BELLINGLISE

Just 40 minutes north of Paris, one can experience the magic of the Château de Bellinglise—an authentic sixteenth-century castle surrounded by 630 acres of gardens and woods. The property hosts a fast flowing stream and two sky-blue lagoons. Entirely refurbished in 1986 into a comfortable four-star hotel, this fifty-five-room château provides the ultimate in an elegant luxury retreat.

The Château de Bellinglise has a warring past, dating back to its construction during the Renaissance. This noble residence was used as a military hospital during the World Wars which saved it from destruction. Its main claim to historical fame is that it was at one time used as a prison for Joan of Arc.

Today, the hotel is comprised of three different buildings: the main château, the *valois* and a cottage. Each guest room is uniquely decorated and thirty-five of the bathrooms include extensive use of marble. Crystal chandeliers hang in the elegant dining room, which is richly decorated with velvet, silk and warm wood paneling.

Most of the bathrooms in
the guest rooms feature
extensive use of marble.

The lounge provides a
comfortable retreat.

One of the charming buildings that make up Les Templiers hotel.

The central building houses this comfortable and cozy sitting room.

Les Templiers's restaurant opens out onto a park.

Boismorand, France

LES TEMPLIERS

A little more than an hour from Paris, along the edge of the Loire Valley and the Solonge, are the buildings which make up the quaint and charming Les Templiers. The main building, l'Auberge des Templiers, is located on the site of a former bloody battleground.

The original building was constructed in 1160, destroyed in battle, rebuilt by the Post Master in 1690, and then destroyed by fire. It was rebuilt in 1799 to serve as a post-horse staging-post until the middle of the nineteenth century. Then it became a farm until after the closing of the staging-posts and the advent of the railways. It wasn't until 1946 that the property was renovated as a hostelry.

At first, only the central building, the "Auberge," existed. It was centered around a paved courtyard and had the characteristic façade of red brick and exposed beams typical of the Solonge region. Today it houses the reception area, the sitting rooms and the restaurant, which opens onto the park. Here the bar area is furnished with authentic Chattam furniture. Other buildings in the complex have the complete storybook appeal. One building looks like an English Tudor with a half-timbered façade, while another looks like a thatched-roof cottage in the English countryside. Flowering plants exist everywhere.

The hotel itself consists of twenty-two rooms and eight apartments, each with a unique personality. Several of the apartments contain a sauna and jacuzzi. The luxury hotel complex covers 15 acres. Surrounding the property are nearby forests and the vineyards of Sancerre and Pouilly, and just a few kilometers away are the many castles of the Loire Valley.

Several of the hotel's apartments feature a sauna and jacuzzi in their spacious bathrooms.

The exposed wood beams of the restaurant are characteristic of its architectural history.

Each of the twenty-two rooms and eight apartments of Les Templiers have their own unique personality.

A sitting area features an exposed beamed ceiling.

In the heart of Provençe sits the authentic eighteenth-century Château de Vergières.

Saint Martin de Crau, France

CHÂTEAU DE VERGIÈRES

In the heart of Provençe sits Château de Vergières, an authentic eighteenth-century château with a six-room guest house. Built by an aristocratic family, many of whom were mayors of the neighboring town of Arles, the traditional style French château offers a warm welcome to a select number of guests.

The hotel itself lies in a quiet 865-acre estate bordered by a 700-acre farm and surrounded by meadows and hundred-year-old trees. The guest house is located in the heart of an unusual geographic anomaly so remarkable that it was cited in Greek legends. Today it is known as the last *desertic steppe* of Europe.

Guests of the château are treated more like friends of the owners, who personally receive each visitor. Each evening dinner is served at the table d'hôte as it is in all traditional French families. Here the conversation turns to family life, French traditions, jobs, European politics and in particular, Provençe. The furnishings are personal family antiques and the cuisine is not the traditional cooking found in French restaurants, but rather the cooking you find in the family homes. Many of the guests feel such a part of this family that they become friends who return again and again. It is this special treatment that makes the hotel unique.

Each evening, dinner is served at the table d' hôte, as it is in all traditional French families.

The entry façade of Les Crayères features the typical French château style of the turn of the century.

Les Crayères features a mix of French and English eighteenth- and nineteenth-century furniture and paintings.

The Château Les Crayères features three different restaurants, all fashioned by French designer Pierre Yves Rochon.

Reims, France

Château Les Crayères

The Château Les Crayères overlooks the city of Reims from 50 acres of parkland. It was built at the turn of the century as a private residence, but today is a nineteen-room hotel, run by the famous chef Gerard Boyer and his wife, Elayne.

Although the park was built around 1885, a château wasn't constructed on the property until 1904. It was Louise Pommery, the Marquess of Polignac (of Pommery champagne fame), who built the château in the traditional French style of the day as a family residence. The German army destroyed a part of the home and turned it into artillery redoubts called Fort Pommery from 1914 through 1918. It was reconstructed and became a home again until the Second World War, when it was occupied by the Royal Air Force. Bombs fell during the war, but hit only the vineyard. By 1945 the American army took over the property and installed a relaxation center with a dance floor. Finally, by 1947 the Pommery family again retained the house and lived at Les Crayères until 1980.

In 1985 the château was completely remodeled by French designer Pierre Yves Rochon who fashioned nineteen uniquely decorated bedrooms, a bar, and three restaurants, including Gerard Boyer's now famous one.

Rochon also designed a metal and glass, antique-style winter garden in the restaurant and fireplaces in the suites. Decorated in the best of French design with a mix of tradition, comfort and refinement, Les Crayères features a mix of French and English eighteenth- and nineteenth-century furniture and paintings. The overall feeling of this château-turned-hotel is one of a family house with old-world charm and modern amenities.

Each bedroom is
individually decorated in
the best traditional
French design.

Château Les Crayères has
been decorated
with a mix
of tradition, comfort and
refinement.

Because of its many
romantic canals, the
village of Brantôme is
well known as the
Venice of the Périgord.

The public spaces of
the hotel include gracious
lounges.

Le Moulin lies at the river's
edge draped in ivy.

Brantôme, France

LE MOULIN DE L'ABBAYE

ocated in the storybook village of Brantôme is
an enchanting hotel known as Le Moulin de
l'Abbaye. Hotelier and president of the romantic
Relais & Châteaux group, Regis Bulot has created this
charming property comprised of three delightful mill
houses, the oldest of which dates from the twelfth
century.

One of the three buildings, Le Moulin (the mill),
lies right at the river's edge, lavishly draped with ivy.
Constructed in the fifteenth century, it once served as
the abbey for the
monks of Brantôme. The stone building with terra-
cotta roof still resembles its original architecture. La
Maison du Meunier (the miller's house) lies just below
the grottoes and resembles a typical château of the
Périgord region. La Maison de l'Abbé (the abbot's
house) is one of the oldest houses of the village, tracing
its roots to the twelfth century. Here lived Pierre de
Bourdeilles, the abbot of Brantôme and author of the
French classic "Vie des Dames Galantes."

Guest rooms feature elaborate, traditional rich styling with period pieces.

Because of its many romantic canals, the village of Brantôme is well known as the Venice of the Périgord. It is this idyllic landscape, surrounded by pre-historic caves, mansions and châteaux, that comprises a picturesque setting for Le Moulin de L'Abbaye.

Fastidiously decorated by Jean Dive, the hotel's public spaces include gracious lounges and a restaurant styled in the local decor. The twenty guest rooms, most of which were refurbished in 1991, feature elaborate, traditional rich styling with period pieces and chintz fabrics that are sophisticated rather than country cute. Handmade rugs cover the old stone floors.

Enhanced by a gourmet restaurant, the ambiance at Le Moulin de l'Abbaye provides countless pleasures. Guests can participate in a variety of river activities including canoeing, kayaking and fishing.

The guest rooms' chintz fabrics are sophisticated rather than country cute.

A bathroom in the luxurious Moulin de l'Abbaye.

The château's restaurant is styled in the local decor.

The lounge of the Château Cordeillan-Bages features family-owned antiques and comfortable upholstered furnishings.

The mansion resides in the heart of the world's most famous Pauillac wine region.

Pauillac, France

CHÂTEAU CORDEILLAN-BAGES

This seventeenth-century French château is located in the heart of the famous Medoc Wine Region on 5 acres of prime vineyards. Situated in the Pauillac area, the Château Cordeillan-Bages has such notable neighbors as Latour, Lafite, Mouton-Rothschild, Pichon Longueville and Grand Puy Lacoste—all who have contributed to the history of wine.

In typical Medoc château style, the building itself is a beautiful, large one-story stone mansion. The only recent additions include a new guest room wing designed to complement the original château design. Today, the four-star hotel features twenty-seven guest rooms, one suite, a gourmet restaurant and a wine school.

In redecorating the hotel, designer Pierre Yves Rochon selected many of the client's family antiques to re-create the chateâu's old-world charm. The furnishings feature Directoire, Charles X antiques and comfortable upholstered pieces.

The renowned wine school,
Ecole du Bordeaux, is
located at the
Château Cordeillan-Bages.

The hotel's dining room
looks out onto the vineyard.

The restaurant of this hotel is a gastronomic
delight. The chef is a perfectionist at marrying food
with wine and he takes great pride in using his talent to
invent new dishes which change with the seasons and
according to his own inspiration. The elegant dining
room of the château faces south and opens onto two
terraces set between a garden and rows of vines. It is
the vines of this famous region that cause celebration
and inspiration for the Ecole du Bordeaux, the hotel's
wine school. Here, budding oenologists or weekend
wine lovers can come for scheduled or à la carte courses
in wine appreciation.

Furnishings feature
Directoire, Charles X
antiques and comfortable
upholstered pieces.

DESIGN CREDITS

47 PARK STREET
interior designer:
Proprietress, Monique Roux

AMSTEL HOTEL INTER·CONTINENTAL
original architect:
Cornelius Outhsoorm
renovation architect:
RTKL
interior designer:
Pierre Yves Rochon

THE BEAUFORT
interior designer:
Proprietress, Diana Wallis

BISHOPSTROW HOUSE
original architect:
John Pinch

CHÂTEAU CORDEILLAN-BAGES
interior designer:
Pierre Yves Rochon

CHÂTEAU DE REMAISNIL
interior designers:
Bernard and Laura Ashley

CHÂTEAU LES CRAYÈRES
interior designer:
Pierre Yves Rochon

CHEWTON GLEN
interior designer:
Proprietress, Brigitte Skan

CULLODEN HOUSE HOTEL
original architecture:
Attributed to Robert Adam
interior designer:
Proprietress, Marjorie McKenzie

GRAND HÔTEL DU CAP-FERRAT
renovation architect:
Wilson Gregory Aeberhard

GRAND HOTEL PARK
architects:
S. Jaggi of Gstaad, W. Schaepper of Boston

GRAVETYE MANOR
interior designer:
Juliet Percy, Pierott Designs, Sussex
landscape designer:
William Robinson

HAMBLETON HALL
architect:
Issac Barradale
interior designer:
Nina Campbell

HÔTEL BALZAC
interior designer:
Serge Brunst
restaurant (Bicé) designed by:
Adam Tihany

HOTEL CIPRIANI
interior designer:
Gerard Gallet

HOTEL GRITTI PALACE
architect:
Maurizio Papire

HOTEL IM PALAIS SCHWARZENBERG
architects:
Lukas von Hildebrandt, Fischer von Erlach

HOTEL IM WASSERTURM
renovation architect:
K.L. Henrichs
interior designer:
Andrée Putman
original engineer:
John Moore

HOTEL PITRIZZA
architect:
Luigi Vietti
interior design:
supervised by Susanne Magliano

HÔTEL SAN REGIS
architect:
Pierre Yves Rochon
interior designers:
Mr. & Mrs. Pierre Yves Rochon,
Jean-Louis Monier

HOTEL SCHLOSS FUSCHL
interior designer:
Firma Hans Eckhart, Altenmarket im Pongau, Austria

HOTEL SCHLOSS MÖNCHSTEIN
interior designers:
Owners Baron and Baroness von Mierka

HOTEL SPLENDIDO
interior design:
Gerard Gallet

KASTEEL DE HOOGE VUURSCHE
architect:
Eduard Cuypers
landscape architect:
Tersteeg from Naarden

LA POSTA VECCHIA
interior designers:
Penelope Kitson, Federico Zeri

LE MOULIN DE L'ABBAYE
interior designer:
Jean Dive

LLANGOED HALL
architect:
Sir Clough Williams-Ellis
interior designer:
Sir Bernard Ashley

STAPLEFORD PARK COUNTRY HOUSE HOTEL
architect:
Bob Weighton
interior designer:
Anne Charlton of Sloane Decorators
Special bedrooms designed by the following:
Jane Churchill, Nina Campbell, David Hicks, Lindka
Cierach, Crabtree & Evelyn, Tiffany's, Turnball & Asser,
Max Pike, Wedgwood
parkland designed by:
Capability Brown

STON EASTON PARK
interior designer:
Jean Monro
landscape designer:
Humphry Repton

HOTEL AFFILIATIONS

Ciga Hotels
Via Barozzi, 1
20122 Milano
Italy
(02) 6-2661

Ciga Hotels
International Services, Inc.
745 Fifth Avenue
New York, New York 10151
United States
(212) 935-9540

Ciga Hotels
International Ltd.
Palace Building
1-1-Marunouchi Chiyoda-Ku
Tokyo 100
Japan
(03) 3284-0854

Distinguished Inns and Historic Hotels
310 Madison Avenue
New York, New York 10017
United States
(800) 888-1199

Historic House Hotels
33 Montgomery Road
Chiswick, London W45L7
England
(81) 747-4003

Inter·Continental Group, Ltd.
Devonshire House
Mayfair Place
London W1X 5FH
England
(81) 847-3711

Orient Express Hotels
1135 Avenue of the Americas
30th Floor
New York, New York 10036
United States
(800) 237-1236

Preferred Hotels and Resorts Worldwide
Suite 220
1901 South Meyers Road
Oakbrook Terrace, Illinois 60181
United States
(800) 323-7500

Prima Hotels
747 Third Avenue
New York, New York 10017
United States
(800) 447-7462

Queens Moat Houses
Queens Court
9-17 Eastern Road
Romford, Essex RM1 3NG
England
(71) 087-6677

Radisson Hotels
Post Office Box 59159
Minneapolis, Minnesota 55459
United States
(612) 540-5626

Relais & Châteaux
9 avenue Marceau
75116 Paris
France
(1) 4723-4142

Relais & Châteaux
11 East 44th Street
Suite 707
New York, New York 10017
United States
(212) 856-0115

Romantik Hotels & Restaurants
Romantik Zentrale
Postfach 1144
8757 Karlstein/Main
(88) 50 20 60 05 6

Romantik Hotels & Restaurants
Romantik Travel & Tours
14178 Woodinville-Duvall Road
Post Office Box 1278
Woodinville, Washington 93072
United States
(206) 486-9394

The Savoy Group of Hotels and Restaurants
Press & Public Relations Office
One Savoy Hill
London WC2R OBP
England
(71) 836-4343

Small Luxury Hotels of the World
Executive Headquarters
21 Blades Court, Deodar Road
London SW15 2NU
England
(81) 877-9500

Small Luxury Hotels of the World
57 West 38th Street
New York, New York 10018
United States
(212) 869-0492

Small Luxury Hotels of the World
21-7 Toranomon 3-chome
Minato-ku
Tokyo 105
Japan
(03) 3431 6524

Solemar S.r.L.
Via Cavour, 80
50129 Florence
Italy
(55) 2181 1213

Most hotel affiliations request reservations be made directly with the hotels.

47 PARK STREET

Mayfair
London W1Y 4EB
England
(71) 491-7282
(71) 491-7281 (Fax)

rooms: 52
restaurant: La Gavroche
meeting rooms: Business center
equipment: Fax machine, multi-lingual staff
special services: Babysitting, laundry/dry
cleaning, valet, and shoe cleaning services,
limousine service and car rental, doctor and
dentist on call
in-room: Cable TV, VCR, fax, complimentary
newspaper, bathrobes, safe, minibar, hairdryer
facilities: 2-minute walk to the health club, equipped with
swimming pool, sauna, gym, solarium, jacuzzi
Children welcome

AMBERLEY CASTLE

Amberley, NR Arundel
West Sussex BN189ND
England
(79) 883-1992
(79) 883-1998 (Fax)
affiliation: Small Luxury Hotels
of the World
location: ½ hour from London
rooms: 14
accepts: AX, V/MC, DC
meeting rooms: 3
special services: Limousine, valet service
in-room: Jacuzzi, VCR
No pets

AMSTEL HOTEL INTER·CONTINENTAL

Prof. Tulpplein 1
1018 GX Amsterdam
The Netherlands
(20) 638-3019
(20) 638-6061 (Fax)

affiliation: Inter·Continental Group, Ltd.
rooms: 79
accepts: V/MC, AP, AX, CB, DC, ER, EC, JCB
restaurant: La Rive
meeting rooms: 7
office equipment: Fax machine
special services: Butler service
in-room: Individually-controlled air conditioning, CD player,
VCR, fax machine
facilities: Health club, gym, sauna, turkish
bath, indoor pool

KEY:

AC	Access	EC	Eurocard
AP	Air Plus	ER	En Route
AX	American Express	JCB	Japanese Credit Bureau
CB	Carte Blanche	UC	Union Credit
DC	Diners Club	V/MC	Visa/Mastercard
DIS	Discover	i/o	indoor/outdoor

ATLANTE STAR

Via Vitelleschi 34
00193 Rome
Italy
(06) 687-3233
(06) 687-2300 (Fax)

affiliation: Atlante Hotels
location: Steps from Vatican City
rooms: 80
meeting rooms: 2
equipment: Fax machine, video, telex
restaurant: Les Etoiles roof garden restaurant
special services: 24-hour room service,
private parking garage
in-room: Minibar, refrigerator, color TV
Non-smoking rooms available

THE BEAUFORT

33 Beaufort Gardens
London SW3 1PP
England
(71) 584-5252
(71) 589-2834 (Fax)

location: 100 yards from Harrods
rooms: 28
accepts: AX, AC, DC, V
office equipment: Telex, fax, photocopier,
secretarial services and conference services—
charged separately
restaurant: Will make breakfast and light snacks—refer guests
outside hotel for dinner
in-room: Remote-control color TV, radio, hairdryer, VCR
No children under 10 except babies
Closed from December 22 to January 2

BISHOPSTROW HOUSE

Bishopstrow, Warminster
Wiltshire BA129HH
England
(98) 521-2312
(98) 521-6769 (Fax)

affiliation: Small Luxury Hotels of the World
location: Near Bath & Salisbury; 2-hour drive to London
rooms: 28
accepts: V/MC, AX, AP
meeting rooms: 2
equipment: Photocopier, telex, fax, overhead projector, screen,
flipcharts, easels (included in delegate rate)
restaurant: Temple Room Restaurant

in-room: Air conditioning
facilities: i/o Heated pool,
i/o tennis courts, golf,
archery, fishing, horseback
riding, clay pigeon shooting
Pets welcome

BODYSGALLEN HALL

Llandudno, Gwynedd
North Wales LL30 1RS
(49) 258-4466
(49) 258-2519 (Fax)

affiliation: Historic House Hotels,
Small Luxury Hotels of the World
location: 67 miles from Liverpool
rooms: 28
accepts: V/MC, AX, DC, AC

meeting rooms: 2
equipment: Provided
special services: Limousine, valet,
24-hour room service
in-room: Color TV, direct-dial phone, radio
facilities: Tennis and croquet, fishing, rock
climbing, canoeing, wind surfing, golf
Children under 8 permitted at the
discretion of the management
Dogs allowed in cottages only

CHÂTEAU CORDEILLAN-BAGES

Rue des Vignerons
33250 Pauillac
France
56-59-2424
56-59-0189 (Fax)

affiliation: Relais & Châteaux
location: 35-minute drive from airport and Merignac;
50 km from Bordeaux
rooms: 27 rooms
accepts: V, EC, AX, DC
equipment: Fax, minitel, telex, connection jacks for portable
computers and modems, phones
restaurant: Good restaurant / Ecole du Bordeaux wine school
in-room: TV, direct-dial phone, minibar

CHÂTEAU DE BELLINGLISE

Route de Lassigny
60157 Elincourt-Sainte-Marguerite
France
44-76-0476
44-76-5775 (Fax)

affiliation: Small Luxury Hotels of the World
location: 40 minutes from Roissy Airport
rooms: 53
accepts: All major credit cards
meeting rooms: 6
equipment: Fax, personal computer hook-up
restaurant: Dining room serves traditional French cuisine
special services: Limousine, valet, 24-hour room service
in-room: Cable TV
facilities: Tennis, horseback riding
Pets welcome

CHÂTEAU DE REMAISNIL

Remaisnil
80600 Doullens
France
22-77-0747
22-32-4327 (Fax)

location: 2 hours from Paris and Brussels; 1 hour from de Gaulle Airport
rooms: 20
meeting rooms: 1
equipment: All the latest technology
restaurant: Dining room
in-room: TV, phone, minibar, dressing gowns by Porthault
facilities: Billiards, ping pong, croquet, pentanque, horseback riding, clay pigeon shooting, tennis, ballooning, gambling, hunting, fishing

CHÂTEAU DE VERGIÈRES

13310 Saint Martin de Crau
France
90-47-1716
90-47-3830 (Fax)

location: Near Arles in the heart of Provençe
rooms: 6
restaurant: Dinner served at the table d'hôte
facilities: Billiard room, tennis, horseback riding, golf, beaches, skiing
Open March to November

CHÂTEAU LES CRAYÈRES

64 bd Henri Vasnier
51100 Reims
France
26-82-8080
26-82-6552 (Fax)

rooms: 19
restaurant: Michelin Star rated restaurant
in-room: Air conditioning, French & "foreign" TV
facilities: Tennis

CHEWTON GLEN

Christchurch Road, New Milton
Hampshire BH25 6QS
England
(42) 527-5341
(42) 527-2310 (Fax)

affiliation: Relais & Châteaux
location: 90 miles south of London; 10-minute walk from English Channel
rooms: 58
accepts: AX, AC, V, DC
restaurant: Michelin rated Marryat Restaurant
meeting rooms: 7
equipment: Provided
special services: Chauffeur-driven Jaguar, ample parking, helipad
in-room: Trouser press, personal safe, bathrobes, decanter of Brandy
facilities: 9-hole par 3 course, health club, i/o Olympic-sized pools, i/o tennis courts, state-of-the-art fitness equipment, sauna, solarium, steam room, massage, hydrotherapy treatment, billiards, croquet, snooker, fishing, shooting, horseback riding, sailing
No children under 7
No dogs on premises
Kennels provided

CULLODEN HOUSE HOTEL

Inverness IV1 2NZ
Scotland
(46) 379-0461
(46) 379-2181 (Fax)

affiliation: Small Luxury Hotels of the World
location: 5 minutes from railroad
rooms: 23
accepts: All major credit cards
meeting rooms: 2
special services: Helipad on grounds
in-room: Radio, TV, trouser press, hairdryer, phone
facilities: Tennis, 18-hole golf course, sauna, sunbeds, billiards, clay pigeon shooting
Open all year
Pets welcome
Non-smoking rooms available

DUKES HOTEL

Saint James Square
London SW1A 1NY
England
(71) 491-4840
(71) 493-1264 (Fax)

affiliation: Small Luxury Hotels of the World
location: St. James Square in London
rooms: 64
accepts: AX, DC, V/MC, ER
meeting rooms: 2
special services: Limousine, valet, 24-hour room service
in-room: Air conditioning
No pets

EASTWELL MANOR

Eastwell Park
Boughton Lees
Ashford
Kent TN25 4HR
England
(23) 363-5751
(23) 363-5530 (Fax)

affiliation: Small Luxury Hotels of the World
location: 61 miles from Heathrow; 57 miles from London; 13 miles from Canterbury
rooms: 23
accepts: AC, AX, DC, V/MC, CB, EC
restaurants: 2 dining rooms
meeting rooms: 2
equipment: Provided
special services: Chauffeur-driven limousine service, helipad on grounds
facilities: Hard clay tennis courts, croquet, snooker, pitch and put golf course
Children welcome
Pets welcome by arrangement

GRAND HÔTEL DU CAP-FERRAT

Boulevard du General de Gaulle
06230 Saint Jean Cap-Ferrat
France
93-76-5050
93-76-0462 (Fax)

affiliation: Relais & Châteaux
location: 20 minutes from Nice airport; 10 minutes from Monte Carlo
rooms: 59
restaurants: Michelin Star rated Le Cap, Club Dauphin, W. Somerset Maugham Piano Bar
meeting rooms: 3
special services: Limousine service
in-room: Color TV, direct-dial phone
facilities: Tennis, outdoor heated Olympic-sized pool, skiing, water sports, bicycling, golf

GRAND HOTEL PARK

CH-3780 Gstaad
Switzerland
03-08-3377
03-04-4414 (Fax)

affiliation: Relais & Châteaux
location: Surrounded by the Bernese Alps
rooms: 93
restaurants: Le Grand Restaurant, Le Salon Montgomery, Le Greenhouse, Le Grill, Grillbar Kaminbar, Waldhuus
meeting rooms: 6
equipment: Full service from fax to secretarial services
special services: Parking, beauty salon, special facilities for children
in-room: Cable TV, VCR, private safe, minibar, direct-dial phone
facilities: i/o heated saltwater pool, whirlpool, sauna, massage, turkish bath, hot air ballooning, skiing, billiards
Children welcome
No dogs in restaurants

GRAVETYE MANOR

Near East Grinstead
West Sussex RH19 4LJ
England
(34) 281-0567
(34) 281-0080 (Fax)

location: 30 miles from London
rooms: 18
Children over 7 and babes in arms allowed
No dogs in hotel
Kennels provided

THE HALKIN

5-6 Halkin Street
Belgravia
London SW1X 7DJ
England
(71) 333-1000
(71) 333-1100 (Fax)

affiliation: Sterling Hotels, Small Luxury Hotels of the World
rooms: 41
accepts: All major credit cards
restaurant: Gualtiero Marchesi
meeting rooms: 2
equipment: Fax, 3-line phone, secretarial service
special services: Limousine, valet, butler, concierge, 24-hour room service
in-room: Cable TV, VCR, stereo, minibar, private safe, air conditioning, fax, 2-line phones
facilities: Tennis, sauna, steam room, spa bath, horseback riding, snooker, fishing, croquet, clay shooting
Pets welcome

HAMBLETON HALL

Hambleton . Oakham
Rutland LE15 8TH
England
(57) 275-6991
(57) 272-4721 (Fax)

location: Rutland
rooms: 15 rooms
restaurant: Good restaurant with seasonal menus

HARTWELL HOUSE

Oxford Road, Aylesbury
Buckinghamshire HP17 8NL
England
(29) 674-7444
(29) 674-7450 (Fax)

affiliation: Historic House Hotels, Small Luxury Hotels of the World
location: 40 minutes from Heathrow; next to Oxford
rooms: 48
accepts: AX, DC, V/MC, AC
restaurants: Michelin Star rated restaurant and the Spa Buttery
meeting rooms: 4
equipment: Latest technological and audio/visual aides available
special services: Valet, 24 hour room service, beauty salon
in-room: Color TV, direct-dial phone
facilities: Indoor pool, tennis, sauna, steam room, whirlpool, spa bath, gymnasium, lake
Children welcome
Pets in rooms only

HINTLESHAM HALL

(Hintlesham Hall Ltd.)
Hintlesham, Ipswich
Suffolk IP8 3NS
England
(04) 738-7334
(04) 738-7463 (Fax)

affiliation: Small Luxury Hotels of the World
location: 2 hours from London; 1 hour from Stansted Airport; 12 minutes from Ipswich Station
rooms: 33
accepts: AX, DC, AC, V/MC
restaurants: 3 dining rooms
meeting rooms: 4
special services: Limousine, valet, 24-hour room service, ample parking, helipad
in-room: Remote-control color TV, minibar, radio, hairdryer, bathrobes, iced mineral water, direct-dial phones, alarm clock, a "profusion of toiletries"
facilities: Tennis, 18-hole golf course, outdoor heated pool, sauna, spa bath, steam room, croquet, fishing, clay pigeon shooting, billiards
Pets welcome

HÔTEL BALZAC

6 rue Balzac
75008 Paris
France
(1) 45-61-9722
(1) 42-25-2482 (Fax)

affiliation: Small Luxury Hotels of the World
location: Off the Champs-Elysées; close to the Arc de Triomphe
rooms: 70
accepts: AX, V/MC, DC
restaurant: Bicé
office equipment: Secretarial services
special services: Limousine, valet, and concierge service, express laundry, 24-hour room service, private parking garage
in-room: Remote-control color cable TV, minibar, air conditioning, radio, direct-dial phone
Pets welcome

HOTEL CIPRIANI

30100 Venice
Italy
(41) 520-7744
(41) 520-3930 (Fax)

location: In the "heart of Venice"
rooms: 95
restaurant: 2

meeting rooms: Several
special services: 24-hour room service
in-room: Air conditioning, jacuzzi, cable TV, radio, minibar, bathrobes, hairdryer
facilities: Clay tennis courts, i/o swimming pool, spa and fitness
Open only from March 19 to November 7

HOTEL GOLDENER HIRSCH

Getreidegasse 37
A-5020 Salzburg
Austria
(66) 284-8511
(66) 284-8517 (Fax)

affiliation: Ciga Hotels
location: Steps from the birthplace of Mozart in the center of Salzburg
rooms: 73
accepts: AX, V/MC, DC, JCB
restaurants: Hotel's restaurant is good; the Herzel restaurant is next door
meeting rooms: 4
equipment: Telex, fax
special services: Aviation jets, theater tickets
in-room: Color TV, radio, 3 phone lines, air conditioning

HOTEL GRITTI PALACE

Campo S. Maria del Giglio, 2467
30124 Venice
Italy
(41) 79-4611
(41) 52-0942 (Fax)

affiliation: Ciga Hotels
location: Overlooks the Grand Canal
rooms: 93
accepts: AX, V/MC, AC, DC
restaurant: The Gritti Restaurant
equipment: Secretarial services and business equipment provided
facilities: Private sporting facilities

HOTEL IM PALAIS SCHWARZENBERG

Schwazenbergplatz 9
A-1030 Vienna
Austria
(22) 278-4515
(22) 278-4714 (Fax)

location: 10-minute walk to State Opera
rooms: 38
restaurant: The Terrace Restaurant
facilities: 5 tennis courts, croquet lawn

HOTEL IM WASSERTURM

Kaygasse 2
D-5000 Colonge 1
Germany
(022) 12008000
(022) 12008888 (Fax)

rooms: 90
accepts: AX, DC, V/MC
restaurant: Restaurant with roof terrace
meeting rooms: Seat 2-200 people
equipment: Secretarial service, video, flip chart, overhead projector
special services: Chauffeur-driven limousine, 90-space parking garage with attendant and car wash, 24-hour shoe cleaning service, dog sitter
in-room: TV, radio, private safe, heated towel rack, video surveillance
facilities: Golf, swimming, tennis, skiing, sauna, solarium, massage
Children and pets welcome

HOTEL PITRIZZA

07020 Porto Cervo
Costa Smerelda (Sardinia)
Italy
(07) 899-1500
(07) 899-1629 (Fax)

affiliation: Ciga Hotels
location: Sardinia
rooms: 12 villas; 4-6 bedrooms per villa
accepts: AX, DC, V/MC
restaurant: Good restaurant with piano bar
in-room: Private terrace, garden on patio, air conditioning
facilities: Seawater swimming pool cut into the rocks, tennis courts, jetty for small yachts, 18-hole (par 72) golf course

HÔTEL SAN REGIS

12 rue Jean Goujon
75008 Paris
France
(1) 4359-4190
(1) 4561-0548 (Fax)

location: A block away from the Champs-Elysées and Avenue Montaigne
rooms: 44 rooms
restaurant: Elegant restaurant and bar
in-room: Air conditioning, cable TV, direct-dial phone, music

HOTEL SCHLOSS FUSCHL

A-5322 Hoi bei Salzburg
Austria
(62) 292-2530
(62) 292-253531 (Fax)

location: 25 km from Salzburg Airport
rooms: 84
restaurants: Yellow, Rose & Blue Salon, Wintergarden, Terrace (summer)
meeting rooms: 4
equipment: Modern conference technology
facilities: Swimming pool, whirlpool, sauna, skiing, beach, tennis court, 9-hole golf course, boating, fishing, sailing, bowling, shooting, The Lancaster Beauty Farm

HOTEL SCHLOSS MÖNCHSTEIN

City Center, Mönchsberg Park 26-V
A-5020 Salzburg
Austria
(66) 284-8550
(66) 284-8559 (Fax)

affiliation: Relais & Châteaux
location: 10 minute walk to Old Main Street in Salzburg
rooms: 17 rooms
accepts: DC, V/MC, AC, EC, ER, AP
restaurant: Paris Lodron
meeting rooms: Executive meetings (40 maximum); weddings, banquets (100 maximum)
equipment: Fax at front desk
special services: Laundy, dry cleaning
in-room: Telephone, radio, color TV, minibar, in-room safe, built-in hairdryer, private bathroom
facilities: Tennis, well-groomed relaxation lawn, jogging
Wedding chapel Hochzeitskapelle dates back to sixteenth century

HOTEL SPLENDIDO

(Splendido Portofino)
13, viale Baratta
16034 Portofino
Italy
(18) 526-9551/2
(18) 526-9614 (Fax)

location: On the Italian Riviera; 45 minutes from Genoa Airport
rooms: 63
accepts: Travelers cheques, cash, AX, CB, V
restaurants: The panoramic outdoor La Terraza (1 indoor restaurant)
meeting rooms: 2
equipment: Secretarial service
special services: Laundry/dry cleaning service, babysitting service, car rental, 24-hour room service, parking garage
in-room: Color TV, direct-dial phone, jacuzzi, whirlpool bath, private safe, air conditioning, minibar, hairdryer
facilities: Heated pool, private tennis courts, sauna, solarium, water skiing, golf course and horseback riding
Children welcome

HUNTING LODGE DE MOOKERHEIDE

Heumensebaan 2
6584 CL Molenhoek, Holland
The Netherlands
(08) 058-3035
(08) 058-4355 (Fax)

location: In the foothills of the German State Forest
rooms: 7
restaurants: The Baron van Luden à la carte restaurant, The William of Orange Room
meeting rooms: 9 rooms with facilities for up to 250 people
in-room: Jacuzzi
facilities: Golf course

KASTEEL DE HOOGE VUURSCHE

Hilversumestraateeg 14
3744 KC Baarn, Holland
The Netherlands
(21) 541-2541
(21) 542-3288 (Fax)

rooms: 20
restaurant: "Georgette" opens onto the terrace in warm weather
meeting rooms: 5 function rooms
special services: 220-car parking garage
facilities: Exhibitions, theatrical dinners, concerts

THE LANCASTER

7 rue de Berri
Paris 75008
France
(1) 4359-9043
(1) 4289-2271 (Fax)

affiliation: The Savoy Group of Hotels and Restaurants, Small Luxury Hotels of the World
location: Moments from the Eiffel Tower and the Louvre; 45 minutes from Charles de Gaulle Airport
rooms: 66
accepts: AC, AP, JCB
restaurant: 1 restaurant opens into the garden in the summertime
meeting rooms: 2
special services: Laundry/dry cleaning service, limousine, valet service, private underground garage, 24-hour room service
in-room: Radio, direct-dial phone, cable TV
Children welcome
Pets welcome by prior arrangement

LA POSTA VECCHIA

00055 Palo Laziale
Italy
(06) 994-9501
(06) 994-9507 (Fax)

affiliation: Relais & Châteaux
location: 20 minutes from Fuimano airport (on the Mediterranean)
rooms: 17
accepts: AX, DC, V/MC, EC, AP, JCB
restaurant: Cuisine de Grand Mirello
meeting rooms: 1
equipment: Provided
special services: Limousine, car rental
facilities: Indoor pool, private beach, horseback riding, park, golf (20 minutes and 40 minutes away)

LE MOULIN DE L'ABBAYE

1, route de Bourdeilles
24310 Brantôme-en-Périgord
France
53-05-8022
53-05-7527 (Fax)

affiliation: Relais & Châteaux
location: 27 kms northwest of Periguex
rooms: 20 rooms
accepts: V, EC, AX, DC
Open May to October

LE RICHEMOND

Jardin Brunswick
1211 Geneva 1
Switzerland
(22) 731-1400
(22) 731-6709 (Fax)

affiliation: Relais & Châteaux
location: Near Lake Geneva
rooms: 99
accepts: V, EC, AX, DC, JCB
restaurant: Le Gentilhomme, Le Jardin
meeting rooms: 5
special services: Chauffeur-driven Rolls Royce, 24-hour room
   service, private parking, massage, beauty salon

LES TEMPLIERS

Les Bezards
45290 Boismorand
France
3831-8001
3831-8541 (Fax)

affiliation: Relais & Châteaux
location: Minutes from the Loire Valley
rooms: 22 rooms; 8 apartments
accepts: V, EC, AX, DC
restaurant: Luxury four-star, Michelin Star rated restaurant
special services: Helipad, parking garage
in-room: Sauna, jacuzzi (in some apartments)
facilities: 2 tennis courts, heated outdoor pool, horseback riding,
   hunting and fishing, museums, golf

L' IMPÉRIAL PALACE

32 avenue d'Albigny
F-74000 Annecy
France
5009-3000
5009-3333 (Fax)

location: 40 km south of
   Geneva and Geneva
   airport
rooms: 99
restaurants: La Voile, Brassiere du Parc, and a third
meeting rooms: 15
special services: Shuttle service from airport at an additional
   charge, beauty salon, laundry/dry cleaning service
in-room: Radio, 22-channel color TV, direct-dial phone,
   private safe, minibar
facilities: Sauna, steam bath, solarium, massage, golf
   and tennis, skiing, horseback riding, water skiing,
   climbing, hang gliding
Casino and Jazz Club (Le Backstage)

LLANGOED HALL

Llyswen, Brecon
Powys, Mid Wales LD3 0YP
(87) 475-4525
(87) 475-4545 (Fax)

affiliation: Small Luxury Hotels
   of the World
rooms: 23
accepts: AX, DC, V/MC
restaurant: Dining room
meeting rooms: 3
equipment: High-tech, up-to-date
   equipment, secretarial services
special services: Limousine, valet, 24-hour room service
facilities: Billiards, croquet, tennis, sauna, steam bath, solarium,
   massage, horseback riding, clay pigeon shooting, fishing,
   canoeing
No pets
Kennels provided

THE LYGON ARMS

Broadway
Worcestershire WR12 7DU
England
(38) 685-2255
(38) 685-8611 (Fax)

affiliation: The Savoy Group of Hotels and Restaurants
location: 15 miles from Stratford (Shakespeare), 90 miles from
   London
rooms: 60
accepts: All major credit cards
restaurants: The Great Hall (summer - Patio Restaurant)
meeting rooms: 3
equipment: Fax, telex, typewriters, photocopier,
   A/V equipment, translation system
special services: Helipad, free parking, valet, 24-hour
   room service
in-room: Remote-control TV
facilities: Indoor pool, tennis, spa bath, fitness,
   solarium, steam room, billiards

MIDDLETHORPE HALL

Bishopthorpe Road
York Y02 1QB
England
(90) 464-1241
(90) 462-0176 (Fax)

affiliation: Historic House Hotels, Small Luxury
   Hotels of the World
location: 10 minutes from York
rooms: 30
accepts: AX, DC, V/MC, AC
restaurants: Middlethorpe Dining Room & informal Grill Room
meeting rooms: 2
special services: Limousine, valet, 24-hour room service
facilities: Sports facilities available
Children over 8 welcome
No pets

RADISSON HOTEL ALTSTADT

Judengasse 15/Rudolfskai 28
Salzburg 5050
Austria
(66) 2848-5710
(66) 2848-5716 (Fax)

affiliation: Radisson Hotels
rooms: 60
accepts: AC, AX, CB, DC, EC, V/MC
restaurants: Symphonie Restaurant and 1 other
special services: Valet parking, 24-hour room service
in-room: Radio, safe, direct-dial phone, hairdryer, bathrobes

SCHLOSSHOTEL LIEBENSTEIN

(Schlosshotel Liebenstein GmbH)
D-7129 Neckarwestheim
Germany
(071) 33 6041
(071) 33 6045 (Fax)

affiliation: Distinguished Inns
location: 30 minutes from Stuttgart Airport
rooms: 24
restaurants: The Cable Tavern (with terrace), The Liebenstein
   Room, and Hotel Restaurant
meeting rooms: 4
special services: Limousine service
facilities: Tennis, 18-hole (par 72) golf course, sauna, solarium,
   fitness installations, horseback riding
One-hundred-seat chapel

STAPLEFORD PARK COUNTRY HOUSE HOTEL

Stapleford Park, NR Melton Mobray
Leicestershire LE14 2EF
England
(57) 28-4522
(57) 28-4651 (Fax)

affiliation: Small Luxury Hotels of the World
location: 2 hours from London, Manchester and Heathrow
rooms: 35
accepts: AX, DC, V/MC
restaurant: Award-winning restaurant
meeting rooms: 4
special services: Limousine service, 24-hour room service
in-room: Cable TV
facilities: Tennis, miniature golf, croquet, horseshoes, basketball,
   clay pigeon shooting, horseback
   riding (lessons)
Pets welcome

STON EASTON PARK
Ston Easton, NR Bath
Somerset BA3 4DF
England
(76) 124-1631
(76) 124-1377 (Fax)

affiliation: Relais & Châteaux
location: Near Bath; 120 miles from London
rooms: 22
accepts: V, EC, AX, DC
restaurants: Main Dining Room, Yellow Dining Room
in-room: Direct-dial phone, color TV, alarm clock radio
No pets in rooms
Kennels provided

VILLA DI MONTE VIBIANO
Monte Vibiano
06050 Mercatello (PG)
Italy

affiliation: Solemar, S.r.L.
rooms: 6
restaurant: Frescoed dining room
facilities: Swimming pool, billiard room, small labyrinth, summer
   theater
Children over 7 and babes in arms welcome
Open from June to September

HOTEL IM WASSERTURM

INDEX

ACKNOWLEDGMENTS

Upon completion of this project, gratitude is in order—for projects of this magnitude don't happen without help. I would like to thank the European hoteliers, both for their cooperation in this project and for providing such enchanting hostelries. I would also like to thank my partner and good friend Lynn O'Rourke Hayes for her positive guidance and never-ending encouragement, and my associate CC Goldwater for her suggestions and contacts. And to my research assistants Judy Garrett and Holly Clark, thank you for helping in the search for these special gems. Always a source of travel inspiration and support are my good friends of EFM. Numerous others provided inspiration including Tom Jackson, Heidi McCullough, Rainer Rohde, Ann Simonson and Cindy Jaskie. Also, an important thank you to Miles Abernethy and Barry Shepard of SHR Perceptual Management for their contribution to the book jacket design. I must also thank Don Lock, publisher of *HOTELS* magazine, for his support in making this project become reality.

I am grateful to Mark Serchuck and Penny Sibal at PBC International for inviting me to write this book, and I would especially like to thank the following people at PBC whose professional expertise and guidance contributed to the quality of the book: Richard Liu, Susan Kapsis, Francine Hornberger, Debra Harding, Joanne Caggiano, Eric Goodman, and designer Garrett Schuh.

Most importantly I want to thank my family. To my husband Will Rodgers and our sons Hunter and Wyatt, thank you for supporting my efforts in yet another project. And thank you to my parents Leon and Suzanne Black, who encourage me to keep up my writing skills.